# 50 Rays of Happiness

## Simple Secrets to a Fulfilling Life

**Niranjan Shendurnikar**

*an inprint of*

**B. Jain Publishers (P) Ltd.**

An ISO 9001 : 2000 Certified Company
USA – Europe – India

# 50 Rays of Happiness

*First Edition:* 2007

All rights are reserved. No part of this book may be reproduced, stored in a retrieval system or transmitted, in any form or by any means, mechanical, photocopying, recording or otherwise, without any prior written permission of the publishers.

© Copyright with the Publishers

*Published by Kuldeep Jain for*

**HEALTH**  **HARMONY**

*an inprint of*

**B. Jain Publishers (P.) Ltd.**

An ISO 9001 : 2000 Certified Company
1921, Street No. 10, Chuna Mandi, Paharganj
New Delhi 110 055 (INDIA)
**Ph.** 91-11-2358 0800, 2358 3100, 2358 1300, 2358 1100
**Fax:** 91-11-2358 0471
**E-mail:** bjain@vsnl.com
**Website:** www.bjainbooks.com

Printed in India by :
**J.J. Offset Printers**
522, FIE, Patparganj, Delhi 110092

**BOOK CODE/ISBN : 978-81-319-0079-6**

# Preface

Great is the quest for joy, peace and happiness and equally common is the lack of it. Scientists and academicians have spent long years investigating and studying what makes people happy. What then is happiness and how should it be secured? Work success, good health, affluence, or fame are seemingly common attributes of happiness but do they give lasting happiness? Happiness needs to be perceived as an inner state of perfect satisfaction and should not be equated with gratification. Though there are no easy answers forthcoming to such issues, happiness is simply 'a cause and effect' thing. You do a particular thing and that makes you happy;

you have to create an intention for happiness. It may be a tender pat on the back, or holding your child in your arms, or a game of tennis, or a spiritual discourse, you get the same feeling of happiness, albeit in different ways. Why not go ahead and do it? Happiness is happiness and it's pursuit is like the pursuit of truth with its relativeness. Happy and effective people have certain lifestyle policies that serve them well positively, truthfully and fairly. We all have the potential to discover the tenents which can guide our way towards self realization, peace, satisfaction and happiness.

This book would not have been complete without the support and guidance from my family and close friends whose suggestions and invaluable inputs have given the book its final shape. Their assistance and encouragement supplemented my motivation to complete the task. Thank you one and all. I gratefully acknowledge the publishers, B. Jain Publishers

*Preface*

(P.) Ltd. for having readily agreed to publish the book and extending their assistance in the endeavor.

Dear readers this is your own book. Scribble on it, write your own ideas and comments wherever you feel the need to do so. Take help of resources whenever you need to explore further. Use the book like you use and relish night cookies.

HAPPY READING !

**Niranjan Shendurnikar**

# Contents

1. Decide to be Happy ..................... 01
2. Enjoy Your Work ............................ 06
3. Keep Your Promises ....................... 10
4. Make Things Happen ..................... 14
5. Connect with Nature ..................... 18
6. Nurture Your Friendship ................ 21
7. Update Your Computer Skills ........ 25
8. Be a Fitness Freak ........................... 28
9. Become a Volunteer ....................... 33
10. Enliven Your Workplace ................. 37
11. Problems Versus Solutions .............. 41
12. Celebrate an Occasion .................... 46
13. The Art of Communication ............ 48
14. Take a Weekly Sabbatical ................ 52
15. Agree to Disagree ............................ 56

| | |
|---|---|
| 16. | Be a Voluntary Blood Donor ........... 59 |
| 17. | The Magic of Touch ....................... 63 |
| 18. | Set an Example to Follow ............... 66 |
| 19. | Relish the Fruity Benefits ............... 69 |
| 20. | Accept the Change ........................... 72 |
| 21. | Adapt to New Things ...................... 76 |
| 22. | Practice Mindfulness at Work ......... 79 |
| 23. | Become a Good Read ...................... 84 |
| 24. | Keep Your Mind Sharp ................... 88 |
| 25. | Flash a Smile ................................... 93 |
| 26. | The Parenting Conundrum ............ 97 |
| 27. | Tied to the TV .............................. 102 |
| 28. | Count Your Blessings .................... 106 |
| 29. | You and Your Spouse .................... 110 |
| 30. | The Movie Magic .......................... 113 |
| 31. | Post Your Message ........................ 117 |
| 32. | Stop Repeating Same Mistakes ..... 120 |
| 33. | Forgive and Forget ........................ 124 |
| 34. | Learning and Progressing .............. 128 |
| 35. | It Isn't That Bad ............................ 132 |
| 36. | Practice Kindness .......................... 135 |

37. Discover Elderly Happiness ........... 140
38. Generate a Sense of Gratitude ...... 143
39. Laughter is the Best Medicine ...... 147
40. Master Your Time .......................... 150
41. A Good Night's Sleep ..................... 156
42. Mellow with Music ........................ 160
43. Rekindle Your Romance ................ 164
44. Life is Like That ............................ 168
45. Money Matters .............................. 172
46. Taming Your Anger ....................... 176
47. Do Your SWOT Analysis ............. 182
48. Meditation, A Delight ................... 185
49. Life is an Attitude ......................... 189
50. Submit to Spiritual Splendor ....... 192

# CHAPTER ONE

# DECIDE TO BE HAPPY

*Happiness is not a goal, it's a way of travelling.*
— *William James*

Who doesn't want to be a happy, healthy, peaceful, motivated and satisfied individual? What are the ways to seek and live happily? How come some people are happy and others aren't so? We tend to believe that peace of mind, good health, success at workplace, family life and wealth would generally make us happier, light hearted and relaxed. Scientific research over the past few years has improved our understanding and practice of happiness. Does money buy happiness? Does fame and success make one feel more cheerful? Does beauty add to the rejoice? The questions are seemingly eternal but the fact remains that no possession or achievement can have any meaning if it does not make us happy.

There are no simple or easy answers forthcoming to such issues. However to put it simply, happiness is a 'cause and effect' thing. You do something at a personal level and that makes you happy. Whether you go for jogging, listen to music, enjoy your work, spend money wisely or achieve top position in your company, you get the same feeling, albeit in a different way. Happiness is happiness, and it's pursuit is like the pursuit of truth with all it's relativeness. There are no hidden secrets of happiness; life remains simply a matter of perspective. The good thing about happiness is that all of us can learn and condition ourselves to be happy.

Happiness is a state of our mind. It's within us, it's a feeling of peace, gratification and internal realization. Happiness is about living with passion, coherence, meaning and integrity, and being satisfied with life. Unhappy people become enclosed in a matrix of self-denial, resentment and frustration. They see every action and event as someone else's fault.

Daily routines, relationships and workplace environment further bring with it, their own kinds of issues – family responsibilities, uncertain schedules, short notice meetings, unrealistic deadlines, fierce competition, unco-operative colleagues and long, tiresome commutes. Rightly so, the resultant stress, frustration, anger and setbacks drain out the physical and mental energies. When you ponder about it, you feel that almost none of these work and family related issues can be avoided. If wisdom, patience and perspective were used effectively, life would become much easier and less stressful for us and those around us too. The optimism and confidence about our perceived, practiced and targeted modifications can help to bring out substantial changes in our attitudes and behaviors.

Happiness is like honey, you can not spread it without getting some on yourself.

Happiness is a way of life. It's absolutely within your reach. Happiness makes qualitative additions to the personality of an individual. It's pursuit makes one a pleasant, energetic, likeable, radiant and captivating person. The chances are that by becoming a happier person one would become a level headed, positive and a solution oriented person. Making this realization within yourself is one of the first steps to start working gradually towards bliss, peace and fulfillment. Do not be moored in a harbor, get ready to make a move and venture out to discover a new person within you.

*The search for an answer to the question of happiness can begin and end with a Chinese saying: Happiness is someone to love, something to work at and something to hope for.*

*—Sudhir Kakar (Psycho-analyst)*

Dr. A. P. J. Kalam was once asked by children on what gave him most happiness in the last forty years. He said, "I get happiness when heart patients carry coronary stents developed in India in their arteries and when physically handicapped children fitted with the lightweight Floor Reaction Orthosis (FRO) calipers find their walking difficulties eased somewhat." These children were earlier using leg appliances which were extremely heavy and impeded their leg movements. Dr. Kalam's vision and initiative brought happiness to thousands of such children of our country. No wonder these heart stents (artificial spring devices in arteries) and orthosis (leg appliances) have been the innovative offshoots of National Missile Technology.

# CHAPTER TWO

# ENJOY YOUR WORK

*I never did a day's work in my life; it was all fun.*

*— Thomas Edison*

Learn to love what you do for a living. Pramod Batra, author of international best selling books on management and an MBA from University of Minnesota, USA says that if you want happiness for a life time learn to love what you do for a living. How true! Many years ago, Thomas Edison believed that the purpose of work was productivity, joy and fulfillment. Unless you push yourself deep into your work and perceive it to be an essential ingredient in making a quality life, then only can you look upon it as something more than the source of your daily living.

Some years ago, I attended a music festival where the renowned violin maestro Dr. L. Subramaniam was giving a recital. I was absolutely delighted to watch his genius and dedication in the performance. He exuded an aura of being totally involved with his art and enjoying every moment of it. His accomplishment speaks for itself. Like many amongst us, I have great admiration for our country's sports stars. You have to watch them playing and enjoying the moments too. That too when they know they are being watched by millions, victory is at stake and pressures and expectations are enormous.

A great majority of us are not high profile individuals; infact, we are regular office goers or business people. We may not be apparently noticeable by people at large. Still we need to make a difference, difference to our own self and those around us.

*There is no pleasure in having nothing to do; the fun is in or having lots to do and doing it.*
—Zig Ziglar

Every work and profession has its own challenges, problems and issues. Whether they are high profile executive positions or mid level managers or non-technical unskilled work, each one has its own set of challenges and problems. Problems and setbacks are not the end of the world. If there were no problems, why would one be needed in the job at the first place? If there was no darkness, then how could have we realized the importance of light? The solution is to look forward. Give it your total commitment, which will bring out your best. Do it with

*Enjoy Your Wrok*

courage, passion and resilience. Once you enjoy what you do and feel proud about it, be assured that you are adding more meaning to your own and other's lives and making the world a better place to live in.

Once you are willing to stay focused, accept changes, realize the power of rapport and compete, and work from your heart, you are headed in the right direction to make your work a calling. If you are not finding peace and acceptance with your work– evaluate yourself. Job satisfaction is also extremely important. Unless there are compelling reasons, don't get trapped in a job that you do not enjoy. Take a refreshing look at your work, revitalize your attitudes, abilities and behavior – you will surely enjoy what you do. Combine your patience, perspective and wisdom at work and you have a recipe for being acceptable, blissful and cheerful. Have the passion for what you do.

# CHAPTER THREE

# KEEP YOUR PROMISES

My reflections over the past few years have made me feel that we are living in a world of broken promises. Words and tasks are taken too lightly and casually. Nothing kills the credibility more than someone who talks and promises but never follows it up. It happens almost everywhere– whether it is at your office, home or community. There is a golden rule to follow – keep your promise to sustain your trustworthiness and credibility – unless you want to lose it forever.

Whilst it's true that you may not be able to keep your words and promises occasionally despite your best intentions, people do ultimately judge you from your track record and not from isolated incidences. Unexpected events, emergencies, deadlines and commitments come up once in a while redefining the priorities. Catch the first available opportunity to clarify the situation and to help the other person understand the situation you were involved with. It's the lack of appropriate communication rather than lack of your fulfillment of promises that damages the trust amongst relationships in such situations. The problem is however, when we say things that we don't really mean and let it become our habit. Without trust you cannot expect a relationship, friendship or communication to progress positively. Once you break the bonds of trust, you will have to put up with an unsatisfactory or broken relationship. A healthy relationship has a strong base of trust.

It is vital that we focus on small, not so important, implied and subtle words and promises. Has it happened with you, that you told your friend that you would call him at a later date, which though unintentionally, but sadly, never happened? One may think such promises ease the pressures, make things convenient and postpone the decisions further. Even though the intentions may be fair, if you do not keep promises, others would believe that you take people for granted and your ability to be believed and trusted takes a beating.

Next time if you are getting delayed do not make casual promises or commitments to reach in time; accept it and convey the message properly; don't say yes when your inner voice wants to say no, and don't take tasks beyond your capabilities. Focus on what really matters, reflect on yourself and use your wisdom. When you promise someone to do something, you better do it. After all you do not want to be rated as casual, careless and unreliable? Make yourself a package of promises, credibility, trustworthiness, action and happiness.

# CHAPTER FOUR

# MAKE THINGS HAPPEN

As we grow into adulthood and continue to mature in our beliefs, attitudes and actions, many of us are made to think and act in a way desired by our friends, family and society. We allow ourselves to be trapped in the society's expectations, status and hype. Others decide what we need to do. You have to become a master of your mind, learn to discard negative ideas, adjust your alignments and focus on the path that you need to walk upon.

Accomplished sports players know of their attachment to the 'sweet spot' – which is a perfect connection between the striker and the ball culminating from perfect alignment, rhythm and timing. Our life offers us ecstatic sweet spots. Why do people miss this? What comes in between? Is it a lack of conviction or courage? Do self created demons in our mind result in the breakdown of alignment of one's mind, body and spirits?

*The only person you should ever compete with is yourself. You can't hope to find a fairer match.*

*—Todd Ruthman*

Eminent personalities such as Geet Sethi, Kiran Bedi, Sudha Murty, A.R. Rahman and many others have their own identity and have dedicated and committed their lives to the pursuit of excellence in their respective fields. They have become icons of inspiration and dedication for the generations to come. Total commitment, focus, discipline, dedication and single-minded pursuit have brought them the glories they richly deserve today.

To manifest yourself fully and to the best of your potential, accept that you are a unique individual with your own identity and make use of the wisdom of your body, mind and spirit. Agreed that we need to conform to the norms of the society and community but that is where the benefits of conformity stop. Your feelings, goals and everything else follows from the decisions that you are going to make and execute. The perspectives and the priorities would help you create the path and purpose of your life. Don't do things to fit in or just to please others. Preethi Nair, UK based author of several best sellers such as Gypsy Masala and 100 Shades of White rightly says that, if you ignore 99 people who say you are useless and listen to one who says you are not, you will end up as a successful and happy person. Be true to your own self and let your commitment, enthusiasm and perseverance be the torchlight on your road to happiness. Work hard. Think positive. Have faith. Be persistent. The process of growth and personal development forms the roots of happiness.

# CHAPTER FIVE

# CONNECT WITH NATURE

*When I admire the wonder of a sunset or the beauty of the moon, my soul expands in the worship of the creator.*

*—Mahatma Gandhi*

Most of us follow a busy schedule that starts with morning breakfast, commuting to the workplace and a busy schedule at office. This is followed by daily chores, dinner and television. Most days tend to follow similar routines that keep us busy and fill up most of our time. How often have you given a thought and taken a few moments to enjoy the beauty that surrounds you? It's still possible to establish contact with nature and it's wonderful creations to help us experience a feeling of peace, serenity and happiness.

After a busy and long day, one needs to unwind mentally and physically to experience relaxation, peace and happiness. Make an attempt to get in touch with nature. Experience the joys of a golden sunrise at dawn, cool breeze, pitter-patter of rain, eye soothing greenery of trees or the feel of grass under your feet. There is a diverse variety of nature's gifts in our country – sea shores, mountains, forests, riversides, lakes and sanctuaries. Though we may not be close enough to all of these, we can still find parks, lakes and countrysides in the vicinity.

Morning sunrise, flocks of birds soaring in the sky, constellations of stars at night, soothing breeze and the swirling waves of sea are a sheer delight to the body's special senses. Besides these, peaceful surroundings always remind us of the divine force that pervades all creation. Utilize such moments to silently thank the Almighty for giving us the privilege to visualize and admire the special gifts of nature.

Explore the natural environment and relish the nature's wonders – take a walk on the beach or a lake side, gaze at the moonlight and the stars and get engulfed by the brilliant colors of the leaves on the trees, their rustle and the pleasant fragrance of flowers. Tending a garden and growing vegetables in your house is a wonderful way to feel connected with nature and to practice caring for living elements. Find solitude in nature's vicinity. Norman Vincent Peale has rightly said that the person who associates with the natural world, thinking of it's spiritually will find his spirit refreshed, his mind cleansed; he will feel stimulated and inspired. Try to live in close touch with nature and feel its presence whenever you can. Refresh your mind and body

# CHAPTER SIX

# NURTURE YOUR FRIENDSHIP

*My best friend is the one who brings out the best in me.*

- *Henry Ford*

Throughout our lives – each one of us needs friends. As we continue to grow, our friendships become precious and important to live our lives fully and happily. How do you feel whenever you find time to spend with your buddies? I am sure that you would feel more energetic, vibrant and happy whenever your trusted friend calls on your phone across the many miles or drops in to meet you and the family. E-mails and cell phones have brought us together once again!

Nurturing great and soulful friendships is one of the surest ways to find more happiness and joys in life. There are moments in our lives when our hearts feel heavy and we want to talk to somebody close to us to share our problems. A recent opinion poll in a periodical, outlook, conducted across the country observed that fifty four percent people combated unhappiness by meeting their friends. Good friends encourage you to do your best, help you to develop your personality and make you feel good about yourself. A good friendship and a reliable social network give us a feeling of strength, security and comfort.

About once every month, I try to meet my close friends for a while. We tend to spend some quality time together–like a stroll in the park, or spending time in a coffee parlor or watching a movie together. Our time together gives us thoughts to reflect on our work, lives and families. Suggestions are exchanged and mutually accepted. Lighter moments are also shared in a funny manner.

*The most I can do for my friend is simply to be his friend.*

*—Henry David Thoreau*

Studies indicate that people with a wide circle of friends live longer, laugh more and worry less. A research study at University of Chicago showed that people who are able to form intimate relationships which are defined as having five or more close non-family friends are fifty percent more likely to describe themselves as happy as those who find it hard to have such close relationships. Like other good things in life, you have to nurture your friendship. Friendship is like every other area of life. It is something that you must work at and keep working on it. Show acceptance, commitment and sincerity and you have a sure prescription for a truly great relationship. Don't anticipate faultless friends. Everyone has some drawbacks. Accept them. Try to mend the faults. Once in a while if you feel that the relationship is becoming frayed or inconsiderate, back off and have an arm's length relationship.

Make friendship a part and parcel of your happiness. If you have friends, you would never feel alone. Friends are a genuine need – don't deny yourself of this joy and go on to cherish this true blessing.

# CHAPTER SEVEN

# UPDATE YOUR COMPUTER SKILLS

The first computer in India was imported from U.K. and installed in 1955 at the Indian Statistical Institute at Kolkata. The Electronic Corporation of India Limited (ECIL), a public sector enterprise began production of computers in 1971 with indigenous processors and imported peripherals. The modern era has been witnessing an unprecedented growth of computer applications in the present era. These appliances have become an integral part of our system, affect our functioning and are here to stay for good. Computers help in rapid processing of information, provide an improved access to literature and have an endless capacity for the storage of information. No field has been left untouched by computers, and computer industry and application are witnessing an unprecedented growth, both in public and private sectors.

The rapid emergence of internet in 1990's as one of the powerful tools for global communication has unveiled new vistas in the information and technology sector. The spectrum of benefits that computers and information technology are expected to provide are remarkable, connecting people together, improving audio-visual presentations, tracking appointments, sales and projects, keeping accounting records, accessing information from remote sources and many more. It's probably time to rename the word library as 'Cybrary'. Thanks to Bill Gates for having made our lives and work much easier.

Whether you are thirty or seventy years old do not let go the benefits of this technology. Be in touch and empower yourself with information. The technology that drives the computing world is changing so rapidly that anything we describe today as state of the art is likely to loose its status within months to years. Keep using computers, keep pace and continue to learn new things to your advantage.

A study published in Physical and Occupational Therapy in Geriatrics in 1996 observed that by using personal computers, a higher level of self-esteem and life satisfaction was experienced by senior citizens. Time is ripe for all to accept that it's a cyber world from now onwards and to get virtual.

## CHAPTER EIGHT

# BE A FITNESS FREAK

*That which is used develops. That which is not used, wastes away.*

*—Hippocrates*

Parth Sharma is a forty one year old executive with a lucrative job, hectic schedule and is always on the go. He continues to work under sustained and tremendous pressure for a major pharmaceutical firm. He is healthy, energetic and a vibrant person, responsible for major decision making tasks in his organization. He says that he cannot do without his daily workouts at the club every morning. His regularity is unbreakable and he admits that exercise adds up to his physical, mental and emotional wellbeing on a day to day basis. There are many more like him who have realized that health is a precious commodity.

Regular exercise reduces your risk of heart attack by fifty percent and also increases your chances of surviving one. Besides exercise also helps you fight and prevent high blood pressure, diabetes, osteoporosis, backache, obesity and arthritis. Changing life and affluence patterns have further led to an increasing prevalence of obesity and related problems in adolescents and young adults calling for an early intervention to prevent adult onset chronic diseases. A study of 18,000 Harvard alumni observed that every hour spent on exercise added three hours to the participants' lives. Regular exercise boosts up self esteem too, making you feel more alive, energetic and vital – physically and emotionally.

There are a number of obese, exercise reluctant individuals who have suffered heart attacks and then realized the importance of exercise, even while being admitted in intensive care units. Wisely, most of them involve themselves in regular walks or workouts after their recovery. There is every reason to accept their conclusion – they enjoyed exercising, felt healthier and slept better.

When you are taking care of your health, you are keeping your energy, vitality and sense of wellbeing intact. You wouldn't just feel okay you'll, feel great. Exercise improves to your physical appearance by adding glow to your face and replacing the flab around your belly with muscles. It would be advisable that you contact your family doctor before launching on a strenuous fitness program, particularly if you are above forty years of age or have a family history of heart disease, blood pressure or diabetes.

Stressing on the importance of physical activity, World Health Organization recommends thirty minutes of physical activity per day. It need not be strenuous to be beneficial. Going for a walk is a great way to feel happy. Jogging, swimming, bicycling or a game of tennis are equally acceptable alternatives and you should decide what you like and relish the most. Besides one needs to be always on a lookout for creative ways to be more active throughout the day. Skip the elevator, walk the steps instead, choose a far away parking space and walk a brief stretch during lunch hour.

One thing that has helped people to sustain regularity in their exercise schedule is keeping an exercise log. After your physical workouts, whether it is walking or cycling you should enter your activity on a calendar. At the end of a month, the sum total gives a boost to your morale and motivation. Admittedly if you are not exercising right now, you may have to push yourself a bit to get started to overcome the initial inertia. Once you start off, you are bound to enjoy it so much that it becomes a favorite part of the day. Many years on you will appreciate the effort put into the endeavor. It would be worth every bit of it. Start exercising today onwards, and have fun with it. Enjoy feeling and looking great and all the very best.

# CHAPTER NINE

# BECOME A VOLUNTEER

*We make a living by what we get. We make a life by what we give.*

*—Winston Churchill*

Our lives tend to follow a pattern – looking after the family, fulfilling the professional commitments, guiding and caring for our kids, assisting our relatives and friends responsibly, etc. Besides, entertainment at home and outside is an accepted norm for an average family. That leaves little time for us to volunteer ourselves to some social cause – unless we look inside our hearts.

Agreed that volunteering time and skills may not be everybody's cup of tea, but as an empathetic human being, there would be some issues about which you would feel strongly about. Countless opportunities exist at every place to help you render your ideas, suggestions, time and skills for a social cause. Let it be an old age home or a blind school, or a toy library or home for destitute or underprivileged kids. Even if you do not have a lot of spare time, half an hour a week should be a good beginning to give yourself to a social cause.

Several health programs and social initiatives such as polio eradication, AIDS control and awareness and female literacy campaigns continue to be pursued with zeal and support from many volunteers. These volunteers and the NGO's with which they work are doing tremendous work for our social and health upliftment. You would feel inspired when you get to know the fact that several million Americans serve as volunteers and give their time, talent and service lovingly all over the world. Remember these individuals are like all of us. Who can ever forget revered Mother Teresa?

Shyam Kothari, aged sixty years is a retired air force officer. Every six days a week in the mornings, for the past few years he is present at a big public hospital, guiding patients to their respective outpatient departments, assisting transport of sick to their wards, helping them to get their medicines supplied and tests performed. He always has a smiling face, with a desire to do something and help everybody. You have to see him to feel his sense of purpose, degree of empathy and affection towards all fellow beings.

*Truth is more in the process, than in the result.*
*—J Krishnamurti*

Agreed that it's wonderful to drop off old clothes and toys for charity but how about spending some time either reading to old or homeless people or playing with deprived kids? Come face to face with the people and kids that you can help. Do go ahead and make a difference in lives of people who really need help and support. Volunteering does not mean giving. It means changing your perspective and improving yourself as you improve the world around you. Feel happy yourself and make others happy too. Give people the gift of your time, skill and service.

# CHAPTER TEN

# ENLIVEN YOUR WORKPLACE

As simple as it looks, it is worth some discussion. This is one of the simple yet seldom implemented ways to feel good. If you keep your office clean, impeccable and fragrant, you would start noticing it's beneficial effects not before long. This need not be an expensive affair. Like me you would also be impressed by the systematic, well-illuminated and free environs of corporate offices during your visits there. In contrast, several offices and workplaces appear bland, dull, boring and depressing. The moment you enter such a premise, you just want to get out of it as soon as possible.

When you make your workplace friendly and lively, there are two aspects to be considered for making it such. Firstly, I believe that it is wise enough to invest a reasonable sum of money where you are going to spend eight to ten hours a day. I consider this as a positive investment for my own well being so that it contributes to an improved work output. There are quite a few practical ways to go about it but considering the requirements you can make your own selections for brightening your workplace.

My office is not expensively decorated but it surely has a pleasant look in and around it. I get freshly cut flowers frequently and put them in a flower vase filled with water to help them retain their freshness and fragrance for a day or two. The fresh aroma of the flowers awakens my senses and makes me feel good. My friends' kids draw nice sketches, cartoons and pictures to be displayed in my office. They deservingly feel happy that their work gets appreciated and when such drawings get old, they replace them with new ones. Well organized books in the racks, a few clean stuffed toys like teddy bears, dolls, awards and mementos complete the decorative list at my workplace.

Secondly, the things that unnecessarily take up vital space, and are practically unused, tend to fill work place with unwanted clutters. May it be junk mail, phone books, old used pens, unused books, stationery; they all tend to distract our attention. Let go the idea that you would need this stuff some day and that's what makes it pile up and add to the clutter. Make a reality check and do not keep something just because you may need it some day. Becoming clutter free offers you more space, saves time and energy and gives your workplace a better, organized look.

It does not mean that enlivening your workplace is going to remove all your work stress.

That depends on the nature of the work you do. However, when you enliven your office it does make you feel good and happy where you are going to spend a major part of your day. Give it a bright, pleasant, neat, organized and fresh look and feel the same way too.

## CHAPTER ELEVEN

# PROBLEMS VERSUS SOLUTIONS

*I was always looking outside myself for strength and confidence but it comes from within. It was there all the time.*

-*Anna Freud (Psycho-analyst)*

Norman Vincent Peale, a religious leader and author of several international best sellers and popularly known as father of positive thinking, knew all about how to achieve a happy, satisfying and a worthwhile life. You can choose whether you want to be a positive or negative person. The kind of person that you ultimately become will determine everything else—attitudes, attributes, abilities, relationships and goals.

While working on an important professional project, one of my co-workers interfered with my assignments, work schedule and did the best to drain my energy. His actions were clearly unjustified but somehow I simply loved the project and was keen to complete it on schedule. Realizing that this needed some introspection on my part, I analyzed the priorities and the perspectives concerning the issues to help me see through the completion of the project. I sat with my note book, listed the problems, thought the questions and wrote different perspectives and imagined few solutions. Few days later I reached a conclusion – what my colleague is doing is not important for me but it's more important how I manage the situation. A cool mental processing helped me to handle the stressful situation positively and now I look back with satisfaction that I did not let go of the right priorities or felt consumed by the problem. You have got to get it straight.

You may feel weak or helpless on encountering a problem. That's human and quite often an initial response. Negative thoughts cloud the mind– why me? This is too tough! That's awful! I am going to flunk this test! Negative thoughts like these dampen your spirits, enthusiasm and the efforts needed to tackle the problem. They in fact condition your mind and body for a failure. But when you analyze carefully and focus upon potential solutions, you still see the problem and visualize the ray of sunshine through the clouds.

*If you approach the future pessimisticaly, then you can be pretty certain the things you fear most are going to happen.*

—Douglas Adams

Negativity affects people physically, mentally and emotionally. You may occasionally slide back into negative thoughts. All of us do. Just remind yourself and switch back into positive mode. When you find things becoming difficult or too hot, seek opinion and feedback from someone you trust. Each experience in your life is unique and worthy; it makes you grow wiser and mature. When you face a challenge, think positively, do the best you can and believe in the good things of life. Great sports persons visualize themselves hitting the shots, crossing the finishing line and shooting the target. Face the problem with an upbeat attitude. Even if you are unable to seek the best solution to every problem, its worth trying to strengthen your self esteem and make you feel empowered. Go online to the website www.optimist.org and find more about positive thinking. Andrew Matthews, an international management expert has rightly stated: *You don't find happiness in the absence of problems, you find happiness in spite of problems!* Never underestimate the power of positive thinking and surge ahead with peace, happiness and a sense of achievement.

## CHAPTER TWELVE

# CELEBRATE AN OCCASION

*A joy that is shared is a joy made double.*
— *English Proverb*

Do you recollect when you celebrated your birthday last? Doesn't making a nice professional presentation boost up your endorphins – the happiness hormones? How did you feel when your daughter's painting drew accolades and won the first prize at a city level event? Get together with your family and a few friends and transform occasions like anniversaries, birthdays and re-unions or winning prizes into well deserved celebrations. Sadly most of us may even fail to take a note of them.

If you start to recognize and celebrate small successes in day to day lives and learn to savour them, you would add further satisfaction and happiness to life. We do not have to wait for the days marked on the calendars. What I am suggesting is that, even small successes can rekindle you and your family's spirits. Celebrate the occasion with zest, share and multiply the joy manifold and keep on looking ahead for such opportunities in the future.

None of such events need to be celebrated spectacularly but within our means. It is not necessary that you have a big celebration. Just take your family for a long drive, or for a nice healthy dinner, or a swim in a pool. There is no dearth of ways by which small yet worthwhile events can be turned into joyous moments. Such celebrations will reward you and your family with quality time, make you feel closer to each other and enhance the feeling of happiness. Celebrate life with those whom you adore most.

## CHAPTER THIRTEEN

# THE ART OF COMMUNICATION

*I have learned a great deal from listening carefully. Most people never listen.*

— *Ernest Hemingway*

It is quite simple but not well appreciated; when people express themselves they generally expect two things; they have been heard and they have been understood. Sincere listening and good communication are mutually synergistic to each other. Good communication is not only about our words but also about our body language, thoughts in mind, eye contact and voice modulation. Everything about you such as your head nods and sounds of understanding give an impression to the listener that you listen and understand people.

People would tell you what they want if you would listen. Good communication and relationship is a two-way channel of listening, understanding and responding fairly. It does take an effort to concentrate and understand what is being said and to come to a logical impression. Whether its day to day work with colleagues, family or friends, do we really listen? Do we let the other person finish without interrupting? Do we continue to let our mind drift and not pay attention to what the other person is saying? Real a good listening requires careful attention and need to clearly understand the other person's perspective. Don't tend to argue, interrupt and put forth your own opinion before considering the other person's logic.

Don't be too quick to comment. Listen openly and with concentration. Respond thoughtfully. You can not be a good communicator unless you are a good listener. Some people are too quick to offer their own opinion, comments and reactions – as if they have something heavy on their chests. Choose your responses carefully and judiciously. Avoid hurting, inappropriate, countering and distressing responses. Reflect and think before speaking – you would feel less distressed, more peaceful and happy. Try to give a gentle pause of seconds before you speak – you will be happy that you did.

The CEOs of leading industries listen directly to the people who make the products and serve the customers. These people go out to the field, listen directly to the customers, who are rightly recognized as the true foundation of corporate power. Whilst there may not have been a formal educational curriculum to equip most of us with communication skills, it remains an essential tools for our daily functioning. Read books, buy CDs, surf the net or join a short course to increase total management effectiveness. Whether it's business life or a social gathering or family life, we need to become more skilful in communicating openly, clearly and sincerely.

## CHAPTER FOURTEEN

# TAKE A WEEKLY SABBATICAL

*Live your life while you have it. Life is a splendid gift- there is nothing small about it.*

*—Florence Nightingale*

The Oxford Dictionary defines the word 'Sabbath' as a day for rest and religious worship. Besides the work, the day to day activities continue to multiply and more things need attention now, than ever before. You need to attend to your financial stocks, carry some of the office work home and keep a watch over your growing kids. That too in a day's works. Though stress is not a bad thing, what is bad is when we allow it to transcend or hamper our tranquility, tolerance and happiness.

Every human being needs to freshen up his mind and revitalize his body to recharge the batteries on a regular basis, time to time. Weekends should exactly be reserved for that. It is a weekly period of rest, relaxation and rejuvenation. Taking a weekly sabbatical helps in getting relief from stress, restore the body and mind capabilities and make one feel happier in every role of life. Besides, you get an opportunity to spend undisturbed quality time with your loved ones–the family. The weekly sabbatical awakens you to take on the world in a better, prepared and peaceful manner for the coming days and gets your body chemicals boosted up.

Jeanne Murrone, a clinical psychologist has rightly put it as: *Some of your most creative times can occur when you are not thinking about work.*

*It's like making bread. You can put all the ingredients together, but unless you put it aside for awhile and allow the dough to rise and rest, its not going to be very good bread. Leisure serves much the same purpose. If you leave some space in your life for leisure, you may find yourself being more productive and creative.* Make it a point to spend at least half a day in conscious relaxation.

A late night bash or a hectic outing is not the thing that you should have in mind to equate with the weekly sabbatical. This is contrary to the very purpose of getting back the simple pleasures that life has to offer. Instead of trying to keep up, just give in for the day. If you can not take a whole day, then take off for a few hours or an afternoon. A quiet time with your own self, a nice family meal together, an afternoon siesta, browsing through books at a local book shop, or a game of your favorite sport can do wonders for your mind and body. Make your own choices and decide what you relish the most.

Just don't get stuck where you are least prepared to be – an overcrowded movie multiplex, overflowing restaurant or noisy shopping mall. Plan ahead in advance and enjoy the break. Indulge your inner lazy bone and rise up again tomorrow, ready to face life. You will be glad, you did it?

## CHAPTER FIFTEEN

# AGREE TO DISAGREE

Few years back, as an argument was just getting built up during a discussion, one of my friends, Dr. Shrikant Mahajan commented: "Let us stop this argument. We can all agree to disagree." It took me some time to realize the value, influence and wisdom of the statement. We often tend to believe in our own ways to resolve the conflicts and arguments. Conflicts, arguments and disagreements are a part of our life. We continue to think that most of the times we are correct, logical and justified. We decide what is relevant and important not only for us but also for others. Our families and friends have their own versions of actuality. Almost no one seems to think that, if the things are seen from another person's perspective as well, all would be well.

The thresholds for acceptance and agreement often appear to be at nadir. Why does it happen so often? I believe that our past and continuing life experiences are greatly responsible for making us interpret the things our own way. This does not mean that one should always agree with the other person's views. There are going to be situations that would demand firmness, decisiveness and absolute authority depending upon the extent of the issues. However, the chances that such situations would arise are far and few.

*There are two ways of exerting one's strength; one is pushing down, the other is pulling up.*

*—Booker T Washington*

Agreeing mutually and reconciling the differences and disagreements and putting the strategy into practice is a different story. One needs to be a strong person to reach out to other people during a disagreement and try to figure out a solution to a problem. The key to the problem is to make an ongoing effort to accept and analyze the situation at any given moment. However difficult it may seem, sometimes it is better to rethink the issues coolly. The perceptions may differ individually but lasting solutions can be achieved by understanding the other person's opinion and attempting to come to a mutually agreeable outcome. It makes it easy for people to deal with you and vice versa. The paradigm shift in this effort would make life more enjoyable and help you to bring out the best in other persons too.

# CHAPTER SIXTEEN

# BE A VOLUNTARY BLOOD DONOR

*There are some decisions in life that only you can make.*

— Merle Shain

If you are not doing it already, practice a great humanitarian task–become a regular and voluntary blood donor. Blood saves lives. Being a natural product of our bodies, there is no substitute to it as yet. It's a great paradox that in a country of more than one thousand million, only a small fraction of healthy individuals donate their blood voluntarily and regularly. The resultant crisis of blood and it's products perennially in the hospitals delays life saving treatments and claims precious human lives.

Even healthy people shy away from blood donation and myths like physical weakness after donation and an unrealistic fear of catching infections like hepatitis and HIV deprive the sick, poor and needy of the life saving attributes of human blood. Blood donor motivation is now-a-days accepted universally as an edifice upon which any blood transfusion service worth its name stands on all counts. Without voluntary blood donors any transfusion service cannot ensure the supply of good quality blood in the right quantity at the right time.

Modern blood banks and collection technologies have made blood donation painless and extremely safe. Dr. Virender Sethi, a

Paediatrician from a small town in Gujarat regularly to donate his blood since the last twenty five years. He has made more than one hundred blood donations. He is always full of enthusiasm, vigor and zest. There are hundreds of others like him who propagate such a noble practice.

The human body contains five to six litres of blood and only three to four hundred ml is tapped at a single sitting. Healthy individuals are able to continue their regular work and activities soon after the donation. Typically, each donated unit of blood, referred to as whole blood, is separated into multiple components, such as red blood cells, plasma, platelets and cryoprecipitate AHF (antihemophilic factor). Each component is generally transfused to a different individual, each with different needs.

If you are a healthy adult between the ages of eighteen to fifty-five years, please realize this call of society. Begin with a positive step to contribute yourself towards healing somebody.

Believe me, this would be one of the noblest deeds of your lifetime complementing your happiness with dedication, reverence and fulfillment. Have compassion for those who require blood. It is the least and the best that you could do. Besides, you can start supporting various voluntary organizations engaged in voluntary blood donation programs and thus make it easy for others to donate blood. Make a group, spread the message and invite others to join you. Make a difference. Light up a candle to brighten up somebody's life.

## CHAPTER SEVENTEEN

# THE MAGIC OF TOUCH

*God's greatest creation is womanhood and there is no greater good in all the world as motherhood.*

— *James E Faust*

Mother's touch to us as kids gave us comfort whenever we were sick, hurt or distressed. All the ages respond to the healing touch of one another but perhaps the most physically loving bond is that between the mother and her child. Whether your life seems to be lacking or you live it to the fullest and whether you are a spiritual seeker or single minded materialist, human touch embraces and enriches one and all. As we grow up, we tend to forget the power of a natural healing experience – the touch.

Medical researchers are continuing to discover the benefits of *tactile kinesthetic stimulation (healing touch)* in forms of gentle still touch, light stroking or massage. With touch and massage, babies have shown better growth and development, paralytics an early recovery and health professionals a reduced burn out. People are now also using Reiki effectively to soothe themselves. Research studies at Touch Research Institute of University of Miami School of Medicine have shown that touch therapy has numerous beneficial effects on the health and well being of human beings.

*All the universe has come from love and to love all things return. For from joy all beings have come, by joy all they live, and up to joy they all return.*

*– The Taittiriya Upanishad*

The media and entertainment industry too has realized the essence of human touch and its healing powers. The central theme of Bollywood movie, Munnabhai MBBS is "Jaadoo ki Jhappi". It has wonderfully driven home the concept of human touch in the minds and hearts of many individuals. A popular comic strip about an elephant and a crow (Salt and Pepper), years back in a tabloid went like this: *Elephant: Scratch my back please; Crow: But where? Elephant: Anywhere, I just want a little loving this morning.*

My experience tells me, you should reach out and touch someone everyday. People love that human touch – whether it's holding hands, a warm hug or just a friendly pat on the back. People may forget what you did, what you said, but will never forget how you made them feel. Life is about people, and spreading and sharing happiness. If you give happiness to those around you, it's bound to come back to you.

# CHAPTER EIGHTEEN

# SET AN EXAMPLE TO FOLLOW

As my work requires regular care of children and interaction with their parents over past two decades, I have observed that my attitudes and actions go on to influence certain number of people around me. Setting a good example is not only an improvement strategy for your own self but it's good for your kids, colleagues and friends to influence them to become helpful, affectionate and positive people.

## Set an Example to Follow

It is not that we do not know what to do but we do not do what we know. There can be nothing better than starting with this practice straight away. Why wait for a specific chance to set up a good example? While driving to your work, does it really require our car horns to be honked repeatedly? Accepted that the traffic is slow, but does it ultimately make a significant difference? Why not carry a jute or a cloth bag with you while going to a superstore and avoid the use of a plastic bags? Why get upset over trivial things and sweat the small stuff? Remember people keep watching us and our actions and it is up to us what message we want to send to them. Such good examples supplement our own happiness, peace and acceptance.

*We forget that the paths are made by walking, not waiting.*

*— Robin S Sharma*

Just ask yourself that after a hard day's work at office, would you become a couch potato and watch television for a few hours and hit the sack late? Do you have the courage to avoid the temptation and get off the couch, read stories to your kids, share the warmth with your spouse and read a good stimulating tabloid or a book? We have untapped reserves of self-discipline – one needs to look inside oneself to manifest the knowledge of self-discipline and get the virtue of doing it. Don't wait for an ideal situation. Start today. Always be on the lookout for circumstances to doing something to influence people in a positive manner. Pass on the benefits of our actions to as many as you can.

## CHAPTER NINTEEN

# RELISH THE FRUITY BENEFITS

In recent years it has been realized that good health and physical fitness is not so much a matter of luck as a matter of what we choose to eat. Fruits and vegetables provide essential vitamins and minerals, fibres, and other substances that are important for good health. James Lind (1716-1794), the founder of naval hygiene in England recommended that fresh fruits and lemon juice be included in the diet of sea men to prevent and treat scurvy, the disease produced by the lack of vitamin C in their diet.

Most fruits and vegetables are naturally low in fat and calories and are filling. Dietary fibre (combination of complex carbohydrates) is beneficial for our health as these are useful in the prevention and treatment of heart diseases and colonic cancers. There is compelling evidence that a diet rich in fruits and vegetables can lower the risk of heart disease and stroke. If you didn't know yet, fruit is the ultimate brain fuel. Fruits have a positive effect on our brains, though the precise mechanisms are yet to be found out. But what we do know is that if we consume fruits regularly and effectively, the brain can recall information faster and more easily. People who eat fruits are often less interested in gobbling up junk foods and ultimately feel better about themselves. Eating fruits regularly can have a mysterious healing effects on human beings.

Make it a practice to keep a basket of fruits both at your work place and at home. If you keep healthy foods such as fruits handy and easily

## Relish the Fruity Benefits

available then your chances of consuming them rise dramatically. Eat them as a snack, between your meals. Rather than being selective about a particular fruit, use a variety, make changes or even make them into juices. It's important to eat a wide variety of colorful orange, yellow, red, green fruits. A study in American Journal of Health Behavior observed that eating more fruits was associated with a higher likelihood of feeling capable and satisfied. Take your pick from luscious strawberries, soft figs, juicy oranges, delicious papayas or thirst quenching watermelons. Reinforce your disciplined eating habits by having fruits and their nectars more often. Fruits are one stop shop when it comes to nutrients and researchers agree that nutrients help us perform better and keep us healthy and happy.

## CHAPTER TWENTY

# ACCEPT THE CHANGE

*Change is the law of life. Those who only look to the past or present are certain to miss the future.*

*– John F Kennedy*

Life events continue to occur which may be inevitable and beyond our control. Whether these could be set backs, loss of opportunities, change of home or workplace or making a bad investment, all of these are a part of life. These keep crossing our paths off and on and we have

## Accept the Change

to learn to live with them without allowing them to disturb our meaningful and fulfilling lives.

If there is something certain with our lives, work, attitudes and money– it is change itself. Our children become older, jobs get changed and we try to change everyone around us. A butterfly is the universal symbol of change and transformation. Starting as a caterpillar that learns to adapt to one way of life, the metamorphosis from caterpillar into a completely different form requires a period of adjustment. Eventually, that caterpillar emerges as a delicate butterfly that provides beauty and inspiration wherever it is seen. The moral of the story is simple– if you find yourself avoiding or dreading the change you may be yourself farther from the new and wonderful opportunities.

How should we deal with changes? Should we resist the change, rebel against it and fight it? Many situations might be upsetting and may not be amenable to change even if you feel that they should be. Or else we use our wisdom, stop fretting and accept the change peacefully and happily? When you fight the change you are likely to cause a great deal of agony, distress and sorrow to yourself and thus miss out on a great deal of joyousness. Fighting against situations beyond your control can only be a losing battle. If your wisdom tells you that you can set the things right without the change, do all that you can if you are confident of recovering the earlier situation.

*Good news— You can change, make sure it's for the better.*

*—Zig Ziglar*

The urge to resist the change is human and natural instinct. You need to give yourself some time to adapt to a new situation. Give yourself some time to adjust. Acknowledge the difficulties of the new situation to help you feel easy, and accept the next phase. Sometimes we ourselves tend to make our changes appear larger than they actually are. Take a look, do careful introspection and identify what really bothers you. Make use of Kaizen– a Japanese management philosophy of incremental change which means to be always ready to change positively.

*God grant me the serenity to accept the things I cannot change, the courage to change the things I can and the wisdom to know the difference.*

*– Reinhold Neibuhr (The Serenity Prayer)*

Consider the implications of the change – immediate or implied and try to see the upside. The nature of life is change and nothing ever remains the same. Accept and appreciate each phase of life, and don't insist that life should go on and on the same way forever.

# CHAPTER TWENTY ONE

# ADAPT TO NEW THINGS

*Human mind is like a parachute, it works only when it is open.*

*— Promod Batra*

Accept that learning and adapting to new ideas is a life long, continuous process. How much change our life styles have undergone during the last twenty years? Did you think a decade ago that the number of mobile subscribers in India would be a few million, ten years later? The great advances in the information and technology

## Adapt to New Things

sector and the electronic media during the last decade have made it possible for us to be in a greatly advantageous position now as compared to the one we were in 1970s and 1980s. Gone are the days of Ambassadors and Premiers; the Marutis, Hyundai and Toyotas are very much with us, now and here.

Mrs. Purvi Bhatt is a successful medical practitioner at a private hospital. You always find her being driven in a car by her husband or traveling alone in an auto rickshaw. When asked the reason for her not driving a two wheeler or a car, she said she felt comfortable traveling in an auto rickshaw since her college days and thought that driving a car was too stressful. She believes herself to be comfortable with the things as they are.

*The real difficulty in changing lies not in developing new ideas but in escaping from the old ones.*

*— John Maynard Keynes*

You would agree that she was just consoling herself for her own sake. Why deprive oneself of a convenience, autonomy and exploration? Do you want to regret a few years from now that you missed out on the facilities that you could have availed of earlier? The answer would certainly be a big no. The minds need to be opened to adapt to changes and enjoy the technological advantages. Make the best and maximum use of technological advances, read about them, ask your friends, browse the manuals and surf the internet. Keep using your mobiles, PDAs, digital cameras and videos to connect and capture the moments of day to day life. If you were to see the images that I have captured by keeping my digital camera handy, you wouldn't believe that I could click spontaneous, natural and innovative pictures ever.

Accept and cherish your valuable principles. Do not hold on staunchly to your firm yet impractical beliefs and make a paradigm shift. Accept the world and the benefits it provides, as they exist. The end result would only add on to your life's delight.

# CHAPTER TWENTY TWO

# PRACTICE MINDFULNESS AT WORK

Most of us spend eight to ten hours a day at our work. That makes it a substantial duration. Add to it, the difficulties, uncertainties, challenges and the resultant stress associated with it. The most important question, however, remains that how are we going to deal with common day to day situations? Do we ignore them and let them build up to dangerous levels or do we respond to them in a peaceful manner to improve our work outputs? Challenging problems continue to confront us day in and day out and the only way to deal with them effectively is by becoming resilient, courageous and innovative in our approaches.

Few day to day strategies can help you perform better at your workplace. Don't you feel uncomfortable on being disturbed by a phone call in the midst of an important meeting? Such interruptions lead to a delay in the important tasks, disturbance in work schedules and are a recurring source of undue anxiety. If you have an important task to perform, inform your receptionist of a "no phone time" during a certain period of the day. Remember answering machines and voice mails very useful at such times; and they make great time saving gadgets.

The belief that we can do the work ourself and may be in a better way, continues to bug even the busy and high achieving people. Whether it is filing paper work, negotiating or doing desk work, we tend to believe in doing all the work ourselves. Delegating the work to co-workers and juniors helps improve the work quality and lets one do what they are most qualified to do. Expectedly, a good surgeon operates himself but leaves the daily dressing of the wound to subordinates. No job can ever be successfully completed without appropriate work delegation.

*The secret of happiness lies in loving well and working well.*

*— Sigmund Freud*

Mini breaks and power naps do wonders for your physical and mental capacities and enhance your work performance. Such breaks give your mind and body nourishment and healing by giving yourself a few minutes. Some deep breaths, limb stretching, fresh air and fluids or a brief walk around your office lets you push a reset button, giving you a fresh start once again.

According to sleep specialists, the human body goes through two-sleep phases in twenty-four hours. Take a short post-lunch nap of fifteen minutes to refresh and recharge your body. You may lie down or stretch yourself on a chair or even put your head on the desk. Power naps, as they are popularly known, are believed, by scientists to relieve the stress on nervous system, boost creativity and improve work output.

Public speaking and speaking to groups remains the number one fear amongst a large majority of people. I recollect my anxiety and stress when I was to deliver my first lecture to a class of one hundred and fifty medical students, twenty years ago. My throat went dry, legs felt shaky and voice became hoarse. Gradually, with patience and practice, I no longer feel the stress and am able to comfortably match my performance to the expectations of the audience. Whether you are delivering a presentation or participating in a group discussion, you must get over the fear of public speaking. Start off in small groups, classes, prepare well in advance and shoot off. Once you drive out the inhibition – it becomes a hundred percent self motivating, stimulating, enjoyable and fulfilling experience.

Obviously these are only a handful of potential changes to make at your work and feel better. Remember mindfulness means paying close attention to what you are doing and why you are doing it. I suggest that you take a close look and start working mindfully and see what a difference it can make to live your life more effectively.

## CHAPTER TWENTY THREE

# BECOME A GOOD READER

One of the best ways to keep on learning, enjoying and spending time wisely is by enriching our brains by reading inspiring, thoughtful and great books. Do not wait for any opportunity specifically to enrich your brain with knowledge. Tuck a book under your arm, while you are in a lounge at the airport, or on a holiday or awaiting your turn while paying bills.

Good reading allows us to engage our minds, exercise the memories and contribute to happiness by promoting positive thinking. There is no dearth of inspiring books and we have to make up our mind to expand our imagination and rise to a new level of wisdom within ourselves. It's heartening to see that inspite of electronic media, book buying and book reading continues to grow, when you see people flock to leading book stores to buy the books to enrich their knowledge. Many bookstores now also invite the authors to meet their patrons and sign their books for them. This is a bonus for avid book readers. Besides, the concept of reading groups and book clubs has started to emerge and these are great ways to stay connected with friends and colleagues.

There are websites on the internet related to reading and one of them is www.readingonline.org. This is a website of International Reading Association and besides reading of traditional print, it promotes the reading needs to expand in forms of visual literacy, media literacy and digital literacy too. The term 'biblio' means books and 'bibliotherapy' is the use of books to promote mental health. It is an innovative concept that utilizes books and story telling to help people cope up with life. Trained volunteers have been using this interactive approach to read to patients and children to promote emotional healing, calm fears about being in the hospital and most importantly, to have fun. Since reading is a habit that gives perennial stimulation, you must keep on looking for books on fiction, poetry, science, philosophy, religion, technology, biography and self improvement skills.

*Go three days without reading and your speech will become tasteless.*

*— Chinese Proverb*

'Dare to Dream', depicts a story of grit, determination, courage, vision and continued learning of M S Oberoi. APJ Kalam's 'Ignited

Minds', Sudha Murty's 'Wise and Otherwise' and Mitch Albom's 'Tuesdays with Movie' are brilliant examples of man's dreams, visions, learning, faith, and the power of human minds. Paulo Coelho's 'Alchemist' is another truly inspiring work and a great story about a shepherd boy who ventures into the unknown relying solely on his faith. There are many great works of intelligent, inspiring and passionate men and women available today with us, only these are just waiting to be picked up. Read deep and thought provoking material and feel connected with their sacrosanct knowledge. Make books your constant companions, only then will we become truly knowledgeable and grow as individuals.

## CHAPTER TWENTY FOUR

# KEEP YOUR MIND SHARP

Good health not only means absence of disease on the physical plane only but also a state of physical, mental and emotional well being. Rapid advances in the field of medicine have greatly contributed to the improved life expectancy. Longevity does not mean that those who live longer enjoy a perfect health. How does being healthy relate to our happiness? Agreed, that health to a large extent is based upon genetics, immunity and environment. Our own awareness and actions can determine our level of mental well being, fitness and energy levels. In the coming decades, an increasing number of people are going to live with obesity, diabetes, high blood pressure and osteoarthritis. While one may not be able to prevent these disorders, the life style and health awareness can certainly prevent or delay long term complications of such diseases.

Logically thus, a healthy state adds to our feeling of well being, concentration, better work output, fitness and ultimately happiness. Imagine that when you are sick or unwell, you lag behind on your schedules, tend to get more reactive and miss the things that you enjoy doing. The importance of a balanced diet, proper hygiene, adequate exercise and sleep to make a healthy lifestyle can not be over emphasized.

*Vigorous health and its accompanying high spirits are larger elements of happiness than any other things whatever.*

*– Herbert Spencer*

Scientists and medical researchers agree that an average human being makes less than 5% use of his mental capabilities. Besides, we believe that with graying hair, our senses lose sharpness, thus making us somewhat dull in our reflexes and performances. Whether such events are a part of our aging or a manifestation of subtle disease pattern depends on complex factors. Studies are continuing to identify and analyze factors that could help us to stay alert, sharp and well oriented till our advanced age. You would agree that staying sharp would supplement your happiness by keeping you well informed and oriented, active and healthy.

Further as you age, it is important to maintain mind power. Be sure to exercise your brain as well as your body to improve your concentration, boost the memory and alleviate depression. A recent study in the American journal, The Gerontologist, reported that people who were optimistic before their heart surgery recovered better than those who were not. Experimental studies have shown that every new experience and idea actually creates new connections between brain cells making it more powerful. There is a good news: mental challenges stimulate our brain to grow and the idea that the older brain inevitably deteriorates is simply not true. Like our body, our brain too needs a regular work up. Luminaries such as Pandit Ravi Shankar, Yash Chopra and Nelson Mandela are just few of the examples of excellence unfazed by age. People who have good friends and are a part of different circles are less likely to grow senile as compared to loners. If you look outwards, get involved with the community, stay in good cheer and eat healthy food, you would be helping your own mind to be sharpened. No wonder politicians, industrialists and actors hold on well into their seventies and eighties.

Physical, mental and emotional health is an invaluable commodity. Manage it well with all the sincerity and commitment. Do not let your afflictions dampen your spirits. If you become a health conscious person and continue to remain so, the wear and tear of daily lives would not dampen your spirits and happiness.

# CHAPTER TWENTY FIVE

# FLASH A SMILE

*A warm smile is the universal language of kindness.*

– *William Arthur Ward*

You would have noticed that whenever you are happy, everyone else around you appears to be happy too. Research has found that a smile is known to trigger the release of chemicals and hormones related to happiness, while frowning liberates chemicals that result in unhappiness. While attending a lecture on spirituality by one of the disciples of Ramakrishna Paramhans Ashram, Swami deciphered into the depths of happiness and the importance of the smile. He said that it takes a far more number of facial muscles to be put into action to frown than to smile. What would you prefer to do? Undoubtedly, smile remains one of the most wonderful, pure and simple human gesture across all the ages and cultures.

We all love and adore young babies, get excited by seeing them grow and acquire few skills. As a parent many of you would recall the moment when your young baby first smiled at you. Developmental physiology has made it such that a newborn baby exhibits a social smile in response to her mother at six to eight weeks of age. You may be delighted to know that this is the first meaningful response, interaction and a developmental milestone in a baby's life. Similarly the return of a smile heralds a recovery from many illnesses and nutritional disorders in children and adults. While children do retain their spontaneity to smile, we as adults do not smile as often as we should.

*A smile can do wonders for your environment—both inside and outside.*

— *Dottie Billington*

Smile is a contagious expression of happiness. Scientists in San Francisco, USA, have observed nineteen different kinds of smiles, each of them individually capable of communicating a pleasant message that often would be met with a smile in return. I have found that whenever I have a pleasant and smiling expression on my face and kindness in my heart, people around me seem to be friendlier, warmer and more interested.

Put this policy of smiling into practice as often as you can. Be on the lookout for scooterists at a traffic signal to return your smile. Young children going to school in their over-crowded autorickshaws are a happy lot. They would reciprocate your smile and some may even wave their hands happily at you. Whenever you add a smile to your compliment to a colleague or friend, it reaches his heart deeply. Smile makes us feel and look better and makes others feel better too. It does make sense to make it a habit to put on a pleasant and happy face. Be sure that whenever you smile, the effect would be positive which would continue to make a difference to you and those around you. Starting today, go ahead and grin as often as you can.

# CHAPTER TWENTY SIX

# THE PARENTING CONUNDRUM

Parent-children relationships have witnessed a tremendous change during the last few years. Bringing up children has become an arduous, complex and delicate task. Many parents feel powerless in their attempts to raise their children. Too much change, too much choice, too many extraneous influences and too little time add further to parental concerns and anxieties. What seemed to work earlier does not seem to work now. Coupled with arguments, conflicts, power struggles and parental expectations, nothing seems to help the parents through these tight spots. Solutions offered by friends and relatives appear like ill fitting clothes – too lax sometimes and too tight at others.

All the parents want to nurture their children with love, tenderness and warmth to ensure warm and affectionate relationships while encouraging the children to develop high self esteem and the right discipline. Many times parents feel powerless in their attempts to raise their children. Inappropriate time management, lop-sided priorities and extraneous influences make further additions to parental anxieties and obsessiveness.

*The only way to raise positive kids is to start by becoming a positive parent.*

*– Zig Ziglar*

Remember, parents do matter in the lives of kids. We are accustomed to treat our kids the way our parents and grandparents treated us. It is not likely to work now. As parents, choose their basic attitude towards life, they can also in the process mould their children's attitudes. It is a learning experience for the parents as kids grow, develop and mature from infancy to their teens. Parents along with teachers are the significant people in children's lives who have an important role in shaping what they are and the type of people they would become.

The time is ripe for parents to accept new age parenting techniques, where conservatism and liberalism go hand in hand, and both freedom and control are exercised properly. Use of essential ingredients – love, forgiveness, discipline, consistency and integrity help to create balance, harmony and a feeling of trust within the family. Children need to be loved and respected. They need your wisdom, guidance and trust. They need safety and limits to be set for them. They want you to spend your time with them.

*We need to let our children know that we understand that we are there, that we love and support them.*

— Zig Ziglar

What's the answer to modern day parenting conundrum? Parents are fully justified about their concerns to raise healthy, happy and successful children. They need to learn, develop and practice the skills of competent parenting. Prepare yourselves to take an initiative – you can not hope to be right by chance. Go to the bookshops, browse through the books, listen to the CDs and go to the world wide web. These are all there to provide you with excellent resources to augment your efforts in raising happy, healthy and positive kids. Dr. R K Anand's Penguin Guide on

Parenting, Zig Ziglar's Raising Positive Kids in a Negative World, www.kidshealth.org and www.aap.org are some of useful guides to equip you with knowledge and information for right parenting.

Children have wide variations in their growth, development and behaviors. Remember this fact and give them some space. Comparisons are best avoided. Build up optimism, be a role model and develop a sense of competency in your children. Keep trying new ideas and improve your parenting abilities. Listen to other parents. The ultimate result would a happy, healthy and well-adjusted family – helping the kids to become the kind of children you wish them to be. *As Denis Waitlay has rightly said : The greatest gifts that you can give to your children are the roots of responsibility and the wings of independence.*

# CHAPTER TWENTY SEVEN

# TIED TO THE TV

Television is a fact of life. 1982 saw the launch of color transmission at New Delhi Asian Games and since early 1990s cable network and transmission became widely available. International sporting events were brought to our homes, watching movies in the cozy and homely comforts became a routine and the ever expanding number of channels added to our excitement, thrill and happiness. We and our families continue to love to watch television, cable network and digital versatile discs.

Inspite of availability of some exciting and informative programs such as those on wild life, heritage, quizzing, analytical discussions and animations, the fare presented on electronic media is largely quite negative in it's content and presentation that they condition the viewer to believe in incredible things. Several programs try to focus heavily on extra-marital relationships, conflicts, violence and alcoholism. Not only such programs are time consuming, they promote negative messages that drinking is a preferred way of life, sex outside marriage is exciting and violence is the only way when confronted with injustice. Such a fantasy removes us from reality, mental creativity and personal motivation. We become mesmerized in front of the screen.

*Television should be kept in its proper place- besides us, before us, but never between us and larger life.*

*— Robert Fraser*

The problem arises once you and the family get hooked to it, it is not easy to get away from it. Just ask yourself. How upset do you get when someone interrupts your favorite serial or soap? Television can be entertaining but it can not be a substitute for warm contact between people. Does your family watch it while having dinner? Clinical psychologists have observed that people who sit glued to their sets have a limited ability to carry on their conversations effectively. Too much of passive information would not be good enough.

More often than not, we switch on our TV sets because that is what we are tuned to do and not because there is something we actually want to see. Even the top tens, soaps and horror shows have become too predictable. Your introspection and self analysis can help you and the family see television less often. Instead do something which would provide you wholesome entertainment, satisfaction and happiness through your own efforts, instead of merely receiving it. Do not turn on the set just because it is there. I am sure that you do not savor every food when you go for a buffet lunch. You eat something that you like and not everything which is displayed. Follow the same selectivity with television. Watch it only when there is something that you want to watch. Use your newly liberated hours to connect with family and friends. Surely there are better things to surf than all those channels, but you need a remote to control yourself.

## CHAPTER TWENTY EIGHT

# COUNT YOUR BLESSINGS

*We are all dreaming of some magical rose garden over the horizon instead of enjoying the roses that are blooming outside our windows today.*

*– Dale Carnegie*

Being happy is a mysterious endeavor; it requires only one thing; to count the blessings and not the troubles. People tend to become unhappy essentially because negative emotions tend to over shadow the positive ones. To be happy we want everything to go our way, we want to be a winner all the time, we want every day of our life to be lit by brilliant sunshine. We are focused more upon worries, concerns, things yet to be done, the past and the future. We keep fretting over what we do not have. While it's true that to want more and to improve is a basic human desire, the problem arises when this desire is due to a sense of dissatisfaction and inadequacy. The grass always appears greener on the other side.

We pin our hopes for happiness in future on the desires. Most things in our life are nice, beautiful and synchronized. Yet we tend to overlook and fail to enjoy these gifts of God to us. Remember that peace and happiness of mind is a journey and not a destination. There are innumerable people with limited resources who are positive, inspired and happy. They do not have big apartments, big cars and big investments but they do appreciate and enjoy their possessions.

They acknowledge the value and benefits of their work, see their kids as gifts, take care of their homes, families and friendships. Value your responsibilities, enjoy your togetherness with your family and kids and see them for what they truly are. Family get togethers at a mealtime once daily whether at dinner, snacks or breakfast is a great Indian tradition to bring your family closer. Sure enough, to be near to loved ones is a true blessing indeed.

By no means, should you stop striving for further goals, desires and happiness. Never, you have to be an optimist. Look ahead for opportunities. Don't get overwhelmed. Let your desires, sense of satisfaction and happiness go hand in hand. *Dale Carnegie rightly asks, "would you take a million dollars for what you have? Add up your assets and you will find that you won't sell what you have for all the gold ever amassed by the Rockefellers, the Fords and the*

*Morgans combined."* Postponing your happiness in the hope of expecting yourself in a perfect situation would be a great tragedy. Instead, choose your own path, feel inspired by your strengths, count your blessings and be happy and thankful for them.

## CHAPTER TWENTY NINE

# YOU AND YOUR SPOUSE

*Our feelings are our most genuine paths to knowledge.*

*– Audre Lord*

A happy and satisfied spouse adds to your personal happiness, improves relationship and fills the home with peace and love. No relationship can be considered more complex than between that of a married couple – a husband and a wife. The things and world around us keeps changing but

*You and Your Spouse* 111

the need of a relationship remains everlastingly present. Healthy and happy relationship between you and your spouse is a no small task – it has been built on your day to day commitment towards each other. Your sharing, caring and listening to each other helps you enjoy each other's togetherness. The task is not easy but it's always possible. We should not stand in each other's way– rather, we should stand with each other. Accept the relevance of this – as more and more females are climbing the ladders of fame, success and achievements. Don't let your 'abhimaan' (pride) and envy spoil this beautiful relationship.

My friend Habib Khan, a devout muslim and Sudha, a Tamil brahmin have been successfully married for twenty three years. When they were getting married cynicisms were abound that their marriage would not last long due to wide religious and cultural differences. Their determination and love for each other has made them a 'made for each other' couple. They have a happy family with three grown up, disciplined and responsible kids. Make your partnership blossom fully, walk together with each other's support and develop into two strong individuals walking freely, side by side and functioning in the best way—together and individually.

Your spouse shares your feelings, emotions and victories. She is your natural support, friend and ally. Constant attention to the strengths of such a relationship is the key to success. Forget the disagreements, leave the comparison game aside, and don't miss out to talk out any problems that arise. Also be flexible, share housework and be open with each other. Be sure, you will always get back more than you give. Let your relationship be an amalgamation of love, companionship, synergism and happiness. You will both win.

## CHAPTER THIRTY

# THE MOVIE MAGIC

*Variety is the soul of pleasure.*

*– Aphra Behn*

Though many of us may not be regular movie goers, a large number of people do enjoy going to the movies and being a part of the fare provided there. Most families consider a movie outing a source of entertainment and relaxation. Whenever me and my family or friends go out on such an outings we attempt to analyze the movie in our own way. We usually come out happy and discuss the performances and the technical highlights of cinema. We also ponder over to catch any useful messages that could help us in our daily lives. Agreed that a large number of the movies may not really add to anything useful except transporting the viewers to a dream world- like situations, but we are able to imbibe something informative out some movies of for our daily lives. Also, resources and film guides such as *Virgin Film Guide,* which are based upon definitive industry data base, have made available the complete coverage of most noteworthy movies that represent key examples of a genre or have some special social, cultural or historical significance. Potential viewers can further access internet resources at http://www.tvguide.com/movies/database.

I also do not miss out an opportunity to visit a movie multiplex or a theatre or an opera on my outstation trips whether they are my visits to our cities or trips abroad. Besides enjoying the movie, I get familiar with the new environment. Well made movies tend to make me feel more relaxed, stir up my emotions and remind me of relationships and family values. They also remind me that a good product is an outcome of a well-planned, well-crafted and well-executed team work.

Some of my all time favorites have included movies such as *A Beautiful Mind, The Jungle Book, Patch Adams, Sparsh, Lagaan and many more*. Such movies have moved my heart and soul reminding me that life is a gift and we must make the best of it everyday. Whether they are old classics or musicals or action flicks, you can make your selection. *The Colour Purple* is a masterful adaptation of Alice Walker's Pulitzer Prize winning novel about a southern black girl's rise from tragedy to personal triumph through the course of her lifetime. *Sparsh (Touch),* a story of a blind school and it's children gives a wonderful portrayal of such children; the joy, the pleasure, the acceptance, and a desire to do something inspite of their limitations has to be seen to be believed. This concept has been revisited nearly after two decades once again in '*Black*'. The human spirit remains indomitable. Keep looking on for box office reviews, make appropriate selections and have a rejuvenating experience.

# CHAPTER THIRTY ONE

# POST YOUR MESSAGES

*There are no great acts. There are only small acts done with great love.*
*— Mother Tereasa*

There are quite a few things, which are simple, easy and economical to do, yet they are not done. The good old days brought us letters, greetings and cards through snail mail and we all loved it. 1990s brought out revolutionary changes into our communication systems—we switched on to electronic mode, relegating the old system into the past.

No one can deny the benefits of electronic communications. A mere click of a button can take your message across continents instantly–this makes our life easy and helps save both time and money. Nevertheless there are times when one feels ecstatic on receiving personal hand written or printed congratulatory, thank you or good luck notes. You would agree with me that we look forward to such communications on birthdays, anniversaries and achievements. I am confident that many of us do preserve such cards for the sake of nostalgia of personal messages inside them.

*The essence of pleasure is spontaneity.*

*— Germaine Greer*

It gives me great pleasure when after a training program for doctors, where I frequently go as a guest speaker or a paediatric congress, organizers and a few delegates send me a thank you letter or a note appreciating my discourse on child health issues. I do not miss any chance to reciprocate to such communications. Sure enough, this takes time to evolve as a habit. Keep some blank cards at home to let the friends and relatives know that you remember and care. Even a hand written post card would do.

There is yet another simple way to augment your happiness. Put a white board in your home at a convenient place along with a white board pen, write a quotation for children to read, look out for a chance to appreciate kids, write thank you notes for your spouse and kids on the board. Complement your wife for the nice meal she prepared for you and the guests. You can use the board for reminders too. Each one in the family can make it's effective use. After all, it is quite easy to make someone happy and feel good. Such small acts enhance the bond between you and the people you value most.

## CHAPTER THIRTY TWO

# STOP REPEATING SAME MISTAKES

*I make a lot of mistakes, but I usually don't repeat them.*

*—Ken Rosewall (Australian Tennis Player)*

We tend to goof up from time to time. It's human to make mistakes. To an extent, mistakes are inevitable and actually help us to learn and grow. Whether it's small like forgetting to bring back the laundry or to complete an important assignment concerning financial matters, mistakes need to be our teacher. The vital issue is to recognize the mistake, make a conscious effort to accept it and seek your own improvements to avoid repeating them in future endeavors. Don't let the mistakes be repeated – rather, examine the reasons behind them, acknowledge and analyze the situation to your advantage.

Organize yourself, identify your potential weaknesses and aim to seek improvement to help prevent yourself from making a recurrence of mistakes time and again. Try to become aware of the problem and make a responsive effort to bring about simple changes in your attitudes, behavior and practices to give you a well deserved relief, peace and happiness. Let your mistakes guide you to do the things in a better way next time.

Do you continue to rely unrealistically on your memory or do not prioritize the tasks rightly? Do you often keep forgetting messages and seemingly unimportant assignments? These all may appear minor events but more often than not they lead to chaos, confusion and frustration. Some introspection is often beneficial and offers surprising yet simple solutions. The solutions are already there – such as keeping a pocket diary, using a reminder menu from mobile phone or writing reminders on a white board. Simple adjustments can help you implement simple lifestyle management lessons.

*Doing little things well is a way towards doing big things better.*

*– Alfred North Whitehead*

Over the years, my experience has taught me to avoid often repeated mistakes such as trying to fit in too many assignments into a single day, getting involved in children's arguments and postponing important tasks to a future day. Bill Rancic rightly said that sulking about your mistakes only leads to the future ones. You are your own best judge. You cannot avoid making mistakes completely, but do you repeat them often and do not try to change? The answer may be currently yes. Never make the same mistake twice. Learn from your past and move on in your life.

# CHAPTER THIRTY THREE

# FORGIVE AND FORGET

*The weak can not forgive. Forgiveness is the attribute of the strong.*

— *Mahatma Gandhi*

If you think with a cool mind, you would yourself believe that getting even is not worth the trouble. Dwelling over what happened, thinking about it over and over again makes it difficult for us to move on with life. An eye for an eye may sound good but it will leave everybody blind. Anticipating, looking out for and enjoying happiness is not a selfless but a selfish act. Agreed, to forgive is a slow and a conscious process but after you apply your logic, discretion and judgment, most day to day situations do call for practicing the 'forgive and forget' policy.

The bottled up feelings of antagonism, grudges, hostility and resentment can only extend our unhappiness further and nothing else. Scientific study at Public Health Institute, California, has observed that resentment and hostility adds to sickness by weakening the immune system and increasing the risk of heart attacks and diabetes. Do you really want to be deprived of your energy, peace of mind and happiness by not forgiving? Do you still want to carry on the burden of anger, acrimony and bitterness? The choice is yours only. Leave this baggage behind and think ahead positively.

When the mistakes are unintentional, a miscalculation, an oversight, don't get perturbed with the feelings of bitterness, grievances and resentment. Forgiveness is happiness. When you forgive, you forgive for your own peace of mind and not to console the wrong of the wrong doer. Anger, hate and resentment tend to crowd every other positive emotion in our mind and are not easy to get rid of. You decide whether you can take the decision in a few minutes or after going through days or weeks of internal unrest and discomfort. Trade off your negative feelings for positive energy, peace and happiness. Become a gracious and a well meaning person to open up your perceptions thereby adding to your peace and happiness.

*Heat not a furnace for your foe so hot that it do singe you.*

*— Shakespeare*

Analyze the gravity of the situation, think rationally and weigh the consequences. Dwelling upon the negatives only drains your energy. Forgive, forget and be done with it. Remember again that annoyance, antagonism and displeasure are not compatible with peace, joy and happiness. The choice, though not easy, will always be yours. Follow the philosophy of Ingrid Bergman; "Happiness lies in good health and bad memory. A bad memory helps us to forgive and forget." You deserve to be happy, so proceed ahead and make that happen.

# CHAPTER THIRTY FOUR

# LEARNING AND PROGRESSING

*We can not grow without learning- nor can we learn without growing.*

– *Dottie Billington*

Our work and professional duties determine life's perspectives to a significant extent. Life itself is the most elaborate book and the best teacher, too. We continue to learn from our past experiences and strengthen our desire to succeed in whatever we do. Learning does not end with our graduation and post-graduation. Learning is a continuous process fueled by our passion to do better, feel well satisfied and thus becoming well oriented towards our goals.

Dr. Antara Shastri is a practicing anesthesiologist for more than two decades. She is an extremely skilled and competent professional in her field and you would realize this if you were to witness her at work in an operation theatre. According to her, learning is a continuous pursuit, sincere effort and a commitment for excellence in what she is supposed to do in a best and most efficient way. The manner in which she handles her work and emergencies so skillfully and smoothly makes one feel that an artist is at work. It assures the patients and their relatives of the trust they place in her. Scientists have found that when you learn something new, it creates more links between your brain cells.

*There is a cure for aging that no one talks about. It's called learning.*

*— Robin Sharma*

When we stop learning, encapsulating ourselves within old ideas and thoughts, we wither. We would never 'know it all' and if we think that we do, we stop learning and progressing. There is nothing better than learning that expands our knowledge, wisdom and skills. Besides, rapid developments in almost every field have made it extremely essential that we keep pace with the advances and brace ourselves up for the future. Whatever may be your field of work, there are no short cuts to learning and ongoing improvements.

We must remain good students throughout our life. Getting updated helps your knowledge, viewpoints, instincts, vision and work practice. Learning shows you the way out of many pitfalls that you may encounter as you go along. Whether it is books, CD ROMs or internet, develop a regular habit to carry on the infinite learning forever. Get familiar with internet. Make learning a joyous and continuous process to chug along.

## CHAPTER THIRTY FIVE

# IT ISN'T THAT BAD

At 2.15 hours on September 9, 2001, I had boarded British Airways flight from Mumbai to London. Boeing 747 had just started taxing on the runway, when a technical snag brought the jet to an unexpected halt. The aircraft was brought back to the parking gate at Chhatrapati Shivaji International Airport Terminal where technical experts were to inspect and rectify the problem.

While the process and the waiting period got prolonged, the passengers continued to remain seated in the aircraft. A large majority started grumbling, groaning and whining. Few also lost patience and behaved harshly with the cabin crew. What was admirable was that a fair number of passengers remained seated peacefully, enjoyed the music on portable CD players and kept on munching the cookies. We remained seated, while the noisy engines kept running and humidity levels kept building up. The jet finally took off at 06.00 hours at dawn.

*Any flight that lands safely is a good flight.*
*- Andrew Matthews*

Sure enough there are times when things are beyond your control. Things do not always happen the way you want them to be. This builds up frustration, impatience and disappointment. What would be the best way to handle such a situation? We should be grateful towards such a technological expertise which makes our lives safer and comfortable. No one wants such a delay. It is a small and a reasonable price to pay. After all, what does one get by becoming fretful and critical and losing calm and composure? By becoming mentally flexible, you would free yourself from anger, exhaustion and a rush of discomfort.

Traffic jams, bad weather, postponements, cancellations and health emergencies are often beyond our control and quite often we allow them to rob us of our peace of mind and happiness. We need not allow such impatience, frustration and anger to spill in our lives. Friends may not reciprocate favors, travelling schedules may get altered or someone else may supersede you in your promotion. Such events are an integral part of life. These are an aberration rather than a rule. Face them with as much ease as possible. When things are beyond your control do not let your happiness be ruined by the events; instead take it easy, play it cool and discover yourself again.

## CHAPTER THIRTY SIX

# PRACTICE KINDNESS

*When we feel love and kindness towards others, it not only makes others feel loved and cared for, but it helps us also to develop inner happiness and peace.*

— *The Dalai Lama*

What is the best gift that you can give to someone? Is it costly jewellry? Is it money? Travel vouchers to a popular tourist destination? Any of these gifts are obviously nice but nothing can be greater than a few kind words and an act of being considerate. One of the surest ways to ensure an ambience of peace, love and happiness around you is to cultivate a practice of being soft, polite, considerate and making someone else feel good. By being friendly, kind and pleasant to people you meet, you are sure to leave a trail of happiness, peace and harmony behind, and making people feel better about themselves and life in general.

Practicing kindness is a win-win situation for all. You would rightly agree that some of the most effective methods to improve our life's quality are quite simple, yet not practiced as often as they should be. My elder brother Arun who is a very pleasant person and a happy guy told me many years ago – it makes you feel good if you make somebody else feel good. How true! May be the idea is so simple that it is forgotten most of the times.

When your kid lost the one hundred-meter sprint in his annual sports meet, what were your comments? Did you say that he didn't prepare well for the sprint? Well, this could have been your biased view about his performance on a given day. The kid would have surely loved to get some kind, assuring and sympathetic words from you to boost up his confidence and self esteem for his future endeavors. Sadly negative remarks completely ignore an individual's efforts and focus unjustifiably upon the results only. Harsh criticism instead of re-enforcing an individual's efforts are more than likely to make hope, confidence and faith shrivel deep inside the heart.

*When you carry out acts of kindness you get a wonderful feeling inside. It is as though something inside your body responds and says, yes, this is how I ought to feel.*

*— Harold Kushner*

Once you start looking around, you would discover that there are plenty of occassions to be courteous, friendly and kind. Kindness is something like the fragrance of the roses. You cannot smell them if you keep running. You have to stop for a while to appreciate and enjoy their aroma. Kindness has similar traits. *As William Feather has rightly written, "Plenty of people miss their share of happiness, not because they never found it, but because they did not stop to enjoy it."* Another philosopher on his deathbed summed up his life's reflections as, *"Let us be kinder to one another."*

Whether you hold the door open for the person behind you, or give way to a two wheeler rider at a busy intersection, or thank the bank clerk, or compliment the co-worker, or offer your seat to a pregnant lady in a public transport, or appreciate the cabin crew of an airlines, you help to spread happiness and warmth to the people around you. No wonder such gestures are popularly referred to as positive strokes or warm fuzzies .

Several nations world over have already started to observe kindness days, conferences and movements in a big way. The idea behind the World Kindness Movement (WKM) crystallized at a conference in Tokyo in 1997 when the Small Kindness Movement of Japan brought together like-minded kindness movements from around the world. Let your courtesy, compassion and kindness define your personality. Kindness is contagious. Help to spread it around. The more you will give, the more it will come back to you. Your efforts to be kind are bound to increase your own happiness.

# CHAPTER THIRTY SEVEN

# DISCOVER ELDERLY HAPPINESS

*It is not by the gray of hair that one knows the age of the heart.*

– *Edward Bulwer Lytton*

Studies on predictors of elderly happiness have shown that age is simply unrelated to the levels of personal happiness. Hub Kittle in 1980s become the only player in the history of American pastime to play in baseball games that spanned over six decades. Steve Fossett aged sixty years became the first person to fly around the world alone without stopping or refueling.

When I go for my regular walks in the parks and gardens, I come across many elderly people taking a stroll or playing a game of golf and enjoying their tranquility sitting on the benches. Similarly, at traffic intersections, I am delighted to see elderly people driving their own automobiles. Dr. M.L. Chaudhury who lived till he was eighty plus was a role model for young people by his knowledge and a keen interest in the field of medical sciences. His energy, enthusiasm and happiness were remarkably contagious.

*It's a good life if you don't weaken.*

*— Richard Carlson*

Agreed, that with advancing age one does need to make accommodation for health and fitness, yet there are ample opportunities to cherish the wisdom and happiness all those years have given you. Your mind, imagination and experience are powerful tools—use these to the best advantage of your physical and mental capabilities. You should go ahead and prove correct the old saying, "You are as old as you think you are".

## CHAPTER THIRTY EIGHT

# GENERATE A SENSE OF GRATITUDE

*Gratitude is the memory of the heart.*
— *Jean Baptiste Massieu*

It is natural for us to take things for granted. Do you take your health for granted? Do you value and acknowledge your family's role in your progress and development? Do you enjoy the place where you live? Do you realize the value of your work? Often we unknowingly wait for unfavorable circumstances to appreciate our life. The idea is to remember that our life is a miracle and we all are truly blessed to be here.

Life is not to be taken for granted. Today you may be in perfect health, but tomorrow you may be not. Today you have lots of money but tomorrow you may have much less. Today you have a job of your liking but tomorrow you may be in a far flung remote place, away from the family? Who can predict all such vagaries? When you start thinking about this, I am hopeful that you would silently express your gratitude to the divine power for all the life's beautiful things. Keep consciously reminding yourself of this fact to value and respect relationships and talk nicely to the people around you.

When you do your work well, respond positively to your family, treat your community with respect and do not demean your neighbour, you are indirectly expressing your gratitude to the Almighty. I believe that many of us have a

## Generate a Sense of Gratitude

worship corner in our homes where we pray and express our gratitude to God for all the blessings he has given us. I very firmly believe that we all need to spare a minute or two every day to silently express our gratitude for all that we have. I have personally found the following prayer one of the best ways to express my gratitude and begin the day in a sincere, truthful and spiritual mode.

*For this new morning and its light, for the rest and shelter of the night, for health and food, for love and friends, for every gift your goodness sends, We thank you gracious Lord.*

*– Amen*

When we start the day with a silent prayer and a lit incense stick, we are not only looking for a positive day ahead, but also expressing our gratitude to our work and workplace. I see humble dealers and shopkeepers following this ritual in the mornings and believe me that we have much to learn from such people. Go ahead, don't hold back the gratitude. Feel gratified yourself. Experience more joy around you, your home and workplace.

## CHAPTER THIRTY NINE

# LAUGHTER IS THE BEST MEDICINE

*Laugh at yourself first, before anyone else can.*
— *Elsa Maxwell*

According to one study in an American journal in American Behavior Scientist, happiness was found to be related to humor. The ability to laugh whether at life's events or at good jokes is a source of life's satisfaction and happiness. Laughter somehow springs from our emotional core and helps us to feel better. You would be thus able to see things more clearly and creatively. Laughter is a release, a great stress buster and like an internal jog. Mental health professionals are researching the benefits of laughter therapy, teaching people to laugh openly, more frequently and cope up in difficult situations by making use of humor.

We need to learn a lesson or two from children to appreciate what is easy to come and good for our health and moods. At a nationwide 'Koi Bhi Aao Haske Dikhao Contest' at Rajkot, Jay Chaniyara, aged ten years, beat 700 odd participants to win an all expense paid trip to Hollywood. This young lad has not allowed his spastic paralysis over-shadow his funny bone. Folk wisdom has always called laughter the best medicine and scientists have noted that while we laugh, our healing body chemicals go up and natural painkillers are released. Laughter also lowers the levels of stress hormone called cortisol.

*Laughter is the shortest distance between two people.*

*— Victor Borge*

Make it a habit to take things easy and trying to laugh off your and your friends mistakes. You would find this proposition more peaceful than worrying about too much later on. No wonder comedy sitcoms, joke books and cartoon strips are so popular and widely enjoyed. Go ahead have a belly laugh and don't worry if someone is watching. Laugh a while and make a healthy difference in body chemistry. After all, happiness is a laughing matter.

## CHAPTER FORTY

# MASTER YOUR TIME

*Time is a sort of river of passing events and strong is its current.*

– *Marcus Aurelius (Roman Emperor)*

We often get the feeling that there is not enough time in the day. We wish that there were forty-eight hours in a day instead of twenty-four hours. The anxiety of missing appointments, assignments and deadlines are constantly occupying people's minds adding to stress, frustration and subsequent loss of peace.

Charles Schwab, an American millionaire paid a consultant US dollars 25,000 in 1936 to advise him how to use his time best. He replied; *Start your day with 'to do list' and prioritize the vital few after picking them from the trivial many.* Time is a peculiar but precious commodity. We seem to have so much of it, until we have none of it at all. If you do not have time for the things that are important, it's a time to look at your schedule.

The key to time management lies in the understanding that all of us have the same amount of time. When you want to make the most productive use of your time, develop a clear idea of how you should use this precious and irretrievable resource. Using time to think and plan is time well spent. If you do not plan, you may be destined to lag behind and feel further stressed. Sensible planning, making a 'to do list', recognizing your biological body clock help you to create a systematic, synergistic and timely approach to the tasks ahead. Some of us work better in the morning while a few may be night birds.

Selecting what is most important can be a difficult and confusing job. Think what is 'must do' and what is a 'should do' task and lastly a 'may do' task. Update such lists from time to time and follow them diligently. Many people thrive by using a 'to do' list. You can make and choose the one, which suits you the best.

*Know the true value of time; snatch, seize and enjoy every moment of it. No idleness; no laziness, procrastination; never put off till tomorrow what you can do today.*

— *Lord Chesterfield*

Prioritizing the responsibilities and engagements is very important. 80:20 rule as originally started by Italian Economist Vilfredo

Pareto rightly says that 80% of the reward comes from 20% of the work. The trick is to identify the valuable 20% effort. Use of diary, reminders, calendars and planners would help you to stick to your priorities. A 'to do' list should be made in terms of priority with most urgent work on the top. To increase the productivity within the work schedules and available time, analyze your time wasters. These are the hurdles that come between you and your goals. Do away with frequent distractions such as phone calls, unexpected visitors and lengthy meetings. There are quite a few managers and officers who have a habit of calling their assistants and secretaries every ten to fifteen minutes. You can yourself imagine the plight and the work efficiency of such assistants.

Every work and project is bound to take a certain amount of time. Give yourself a reasonable estimate of the amount of time you need to complete a task. Leave a little allowance of few minutes as things take usually longer than usually anticipated in most instances. Be flexible, don't be too rigid so that you don't create too much of stress for yourself. If you have to reach your office in time, give a twenty minutes allowance and start early. Always leave space for power failure, traffic jams and unscheduled meetings to avoid the last minute mad rash. Can you delegate or remove any trivial tasks from your schedule? Ask yourself. Are you an 'I would do it tomorrow or later' sort of a person?

Procrastination gets our tasks delayed and makes us feel victimized by the shortage of time. Conquer procrastination. Swiss cheese method can be tried to break this hasty tendency. When you are delaying/avoiding something, break it into smaller tasks or set a timer and work a while on bigger tasks. By doing a little every time, you will finally reach a point where you would really want to finish the task. Tackle a task you have been avoiding. Learn to concentrate on the results and not only on being busy. People may spend their day, in a frenzy of activities but may achieve little. The bottom line is 'Work smarter and not harder.' Focus upon how you would feel when you are done–relieved, content and happy.

## CHAPTER FOURTY ONE

# A GOOD NIGHT'S SLEEP

*Pray before you sleep or read a great poem.*
*Sacred words will clear your crowded mind.*
— *Judith Ortiz Cofer*

A good night's sleep is now recognized to be every bit as important to good health and long life as a nutritious diet and regular physical exercise. The sleep needs vary in different individuals but a vast majority of people need about seven to eight hours of sleep each night to recover fully from their daily routines of 16 hours. Over the last few years, studies begun to link chronic sleep deprivation to serious physical health consequences. One of the recent studies in Archives of General Psychiatry followed more than one million participants and concluded that best outcomes were found in those who slept about seven hours a night and worst among those who slept less than 4.5 hours.

Getting too little or an interrupted sleep creates a 'sleep debt' which our body demands to be repaid. The difference between the amount of sleep we need and what we get is called as sleep debt. Lack of proper sleep affects our judgment and reaction time. In USA, several road accidents every year are attributed to sleep deprivation. If you are over-stressed, you may feel that you need more sleep, but what you actually need is more relaxation. There is also a need to understand the difference between sleepiness and tiredness – the former is a physiological process induced by the release of sleep inducing hormone, melatonin, while tiredness could be the result of excessive work, anxiety or depression.

You would agree that a full night's rest is the fuel for next day. If you sleep adequately you would feel better, work better and still feel comfortable when the day gets over. Don't skimp on sleep. Eat a good breakfast, snacks in between at your work and walk and move around for short spells in your office. A catnap of 15 to 20 minutes is useful in the afternoon as this is the time that the body's natural rhythms dip. Sleeping for longer than 20 minutes puts you into the possibility of moving into deep sleep. Go to bed early enough and don't trade away your sleep to the late night soaps on TV.

*There is more to life than increasing its speed.*
*— Mahatma Gandhi*

Sleep quality gets affected by several factors. If the room is too bright, hot or noisy then your sleep would be less refreshing because the crucial four stage 90 minute cycle of deep and light sleep gets interrupted. Make your bedroom a congenial place to retire for the night. Health professionals suggest a winding down time can make it easier for you to have a quality sleep. A warm bath or reading a book or listening to music are useful bed time rituals. Just remember, besides how long you sleep, the quality and richness of sleep are also equally important. A good night's sleep is the best way to begin your day– get ready, feel renewed and start working afresh again.

## CHAPTER FORTY TWO

# MELLOW WITH MUSIC

*Singing helps to bring serenity. Singing is simply merging into the sound, floating on its waves with a sense of contentment and meditativeness.*

*– Sri Sri Ravi Shankar*

Music has a healthy and happy influence and is as old as civilization. Human beings are believed to have played their first musical instrument, a bone harp and sang some 40,000 years ago. Music moves our inner beings, lifts our spirits and fills our hearts with great delights. It affects people of all ages – a small child turns or twists to justify the rhythm, while the old manage to thump their feet or nod their heads. This is because there is rhythm everywhere. The planets follow a definite synchrony. The earth, the seasons, the days and nights are all manifestations of nature's rhythm. The earth, according to the 'string theory', is a collection of bands of different energies spanning between the two poles.

According to psychologists, music helps in attitude building through self-expression. One of the best example for the same is the oldest system of Indian classical music, dance and dramatics which has ragas for each emotion, day, night and season. Indian classical music has popular ragas such as *Miyan ki Malhar,* believed to have been created by Tansen, Emperor Akbar's foremost court musician. Beauty in the interplay between the instruments and vocals forms a unique blend to help in relaxation and boosting up the moods of the listeners.

Ceremonies, rituals and modern religions are replete with music where it is the primary mean of praise, supplication and celebration. Through chants and mantras, music evokes transcendence to a higher consciousness that inspires, enlightens, relaxes and heals. Soul searching compositions with rich melodies and upbeat rhythms can act like elixirs for human minds and body, giving a fulfilling contemplative and philosophical experience. Specific ragas in Indian classical music have been known to influence physical states including relaxation and sleep. Musician and composer Don Campbell in his book, *'The Mozart Effect'* has referred to the transformation and healing power of Austrian composer Wolfgang Amadeus Mozart as 'Mozart Effect'. The feelings that are generated are of relaxation, tender love and enchanting energy.

Besides being one of the common hobbies, building up one's own collection of good audio CDs and tapes gives you and the family a reservoir fulfilled with relaxation and happiness. Whether it is a jazz, rock or classical music selection, it is a good idea to make it your own collection and listen to it wherever you can either while driving to work, or at home after a whole day's work. Like many others, build up your own personal collection of musical symphonies, jazz music, sound tracks and Indian classical music. Works of great artists such as Beethoven, Vivaldi, Ustad Bismillah Khan, Pandit Shiv Kumar Sharma, Elvis Presley, Elton John, A R Rahman and many others continue to fill our hearts with ecstasy, peace and relaxation.

Research suggests that music has positive effects at all the ages, improves our performances and has a wellness effect on our bodies. Make it a truly unique listening experience every day to take care of your moods and remain at your best. Seek to synthesize your inner harmony with the harmony of the universe.

# CHAPTER FORTY THREE

# REKINDLE YOUR ROMANCE

John Gray author of one of the best selling books on romance and passion – *'Mars and Venus in Bedroom'* writes – "We are all aware that sex tends to be more important to men while romance is more important to women, but we generally do not understand why?"

Romance is a pleasurable intimate feeling of excitement and wonder associated with love. Great love stories such as *Gone With the Wind*, *Casablanca* and *Heer Rhanja* have evoked passion and continued to fascinate generations of people. However, the difference between a man's and woman's needs for love and romance needs to be appreciated further. While it is sex that allows a man to feel his need for love, a woman needs to feel loved and romanced before she can be made to feel ready for a physical relationship.

*The most important thing in life is to learn how to give out love, and to let it come in.*

— *Mitch Albom in Tuesdays with Morrie*

Romance should be a key part of your relationship, deepening your intimacy and helping you to fall more in love with your mate. Romance is not simply about flowers, candy or kisses, but the attitude of love that motivates you to give those things. A recent research study conducted at University of North Carolina and published in Journal of Psychosomatic Medicine has observed that people in loving relationships released more of cuddle hormone than others. Release of mood boosting hormones in body systems makes one feel good and happy.

David Blanch Flower of Dartmouth College and Andrew Oswald of Warwick University after tracking down peoples' life styles and happiness in their research observed that, the more the sex, the happier is the person. More and more researchers are finding that safe and consensual sex can be awfully good for mental and physical health. A good physical relationship can help softening of feelings, improving of the understanding and enhancing the communication between the partners. The more you get to know your partner and continue to grow in intimacy and love, the more the sexual experience has a chance to thrive and get better. All these attributes tend to make sex more passionate.

Make emotional additions to your love account. Simple and spontaneous gestures such as giving your partner fresh cut flowers for no specific reason once in a while, listening to her/his advise and resolving even seemingly minor conflicts before bed time enhance the relationship greatly. Design your bedroom with mild and gentle colors on the walls, soft satin sheets and aromatic candles. Add soft music to it and it becomes an unbeatable combination. Love and romance are God's gift to people who are committed to create loving and supportive relationships between each other. Rekindle the passion and enjoy the precious gift that two people can give to each other when they love each other.

# CHPATER FORTY FOUR

# LIFE IS LIKE THAT

*We are not our thoughts. Instead we are the thinkers of our thoughts. We are the creators of the thoughts that flood through our minds and given this fact we can change our thoughts if we choose to do so.*

— *Robin S. Sharma*

The feelings of joy, peace and satisfaction are our innate requirements. We want the flow of life's events to be smooth, peaceful and devoid of unfavorable events. But this does not happen always. Work should be hassle free, finances should always be secure and the kids should always follow your and family's expectations. Isn't it what we would like life to be ? Life has surprises for us in store. All the times can not be the same for us. Generally our lives proceed with peace, content and happiness.

We can not be a winner every day. In times of low feeling you do not seem to find a way out of the rough spots and see only the dark clouds instead of the sunshine. You are in a low mood. The same things that gave you pleasure and satisfaction in favorable times appear entirely different. You are jittery, impatient and intolerant. Everything, however, small or insignificant seems to be a big deal and burden. Our moods are largely responsible for the way we perceive and experience our lives. If the mood is good, life looks good, if the mood is bad, life appears difficult. It's a matter of timing.

In reality, if you make an effort to recognize your mood and do some introspection, it can help you to enhance the quality of life and bring down your reactivity in a reasonable manner. Mood changes are somewhat inevitable but recognizing the change would do you a lot of good.

*To make the right choices in life, you have to get in touch with your soul. To do this you need to experience solitude, which most people are afraid of, because in the silence you hear the truth and the solutions.*

— *Deepak Chopra*

Analyze yourself. Are you hurt or hostile towards someone? Are there too many loose ends at your work and home? Are you trying to squeeze in too many things in your schedule? Prepare your own priority and 'to do' list. Getting organized, completing the tasks will make you feel better. If you are feeling low or depressed, seek help. Don't face the problems alone. Many of us habitually shy away from seeking counselling. Don't over-estimate your own strength and ability to solve the problem. Besides, learn to identify your own stress signals. Does your back ache, or does the neck feels stiff without any reason? Are you not able to sleep well or peacefully? Has your appetite gone down? Remember the mind-body connection. While the physical symptoms would be real, your mind is giving a signal to your body that you are getting too stressed. It is worth while not to ignore such events and thus slow down a bit and seek appropriate help.

Let us face it. Our mind controls us, determines our moods and sends signals to the body. Remember you don't become strong by facing an easy life. Face struggles head on. Become aware, acceptable and aware of a higher state of your mind. The more you are able to do so, the happier and less stressed you will become.

## CHAPTER FORTY FIVE

# MONEY MATTERS

It's a wise idea to treat money with respect. Money plays an important role in our lives and it is a common tendency that as we earn more, we also want more of it. Whether we are a salaried person or a businessman, everyone wants to keep his money intact, acquire assets and let the money grow.

Financial education or financial literacy is basically learning how to spend money wisely and what to do right after you make it. The good idea about money should be to keep it longer, invest it wisely and make it work for you. The financial success stories of McDonald's, Henry Ford, Naresh Goyal, Azim Premji, Sunil Mittal and many others are a result of their brilliant minds, entrepreneurship, technical brilliance and managerial skills.

*Money can be translated into the beauty of living, a support in the misfortune, on education, or future security. It can also be translated into a source of bitterness.*

*— Sylvia Porter (Financial Expert)*

We are living in exciting times where we have potential growth opportunities and expanding new directions for economy. If we have timely information and are willing to be bold and take some risks, we can convert our money into real power, energy and happiness. Interest rates go up and on, gold values fluctuate, real estate is finally coming out of dumps and the stock market is doing a war dance. How do you decide where to invest your money? No doubt your needs may be less but we need to save now when we can. The first step towards wealth creation is saving. Let your savings become the seeds of your wealth. Strategies such as–to spend less, invest the surplus, setting financial goals, and assessing the involved risks should be able to guide you through your financial planning and responsibilities ahead.

Plan your investments before hand to reap optimum profits and minimize the risks. Think about your goals, children's education, marriage, medical expenses and retirement, and plan step by step. Diversifying the investments, not putting all the eggs in one basket, considering market fluctuations and optimizing short term and long term investments have become increasingly essential to ensure good value for your money.

Never, never lose control of your assets. It was not a long ago *Baghbaan* showed us what a great folly it would be mix together a filial love and assets. People have entrusted their hard earned money to others only to have their trust betrayed later. Be financially independent, secure and powerful. If money is what you want to make and grow, you must make financial literacy a continuous process. Don't earn to spend only. Learn to earn to make your money earn for itself. Let your own financial intelligence make the money work for you rather than you working for money. Let happiness become the sowing of seeds for tomorrow's returns. Let happiness become an assurance of a peaceful present and a rewarding future.

# CHAPTER FORTY SIX

# TAMING YOUR ANGER

*You will not be punished for your anger. You will be punished by your anger.*

– *Lord Buddha*

Anger is a normal human emotion common to all of us. However we have a choice – whether we want to hang on to it or else let it go away peacefully. May be your co-worker yelled at you or your neighbour insulted you, so you yelled back or got even with them. When anger gets out of control, it can be destructive and disruptive at work, in personal relationships, and in the overall quality of your life. It can make you feel as though you're at the mercy of an unpredictable and powerful emotion.

With all the stress in our daily lives, it is quite easy to lose our cool even at the slightest provocation. According to the Grant Thornton International Owners survey, stress levels have sky rocketed by more than one third in 2004. Just consider this: driving home back from work, evening traffic tests your tolerance by its crawling speed . You howl on the slow driver in front of you who doesn't seem to be in any hurry. You, get annoyed at the chemist for a minor glitch in the billing. You just blow your fuse at the electrician who arrived late to repair the geyser at home. While some of the situations may call for immediate correction, most of the day to day situations can be easily managed with self thoughts, introspections and patience. It's a time for reality check.

Research at John Hopkins University of USA has analyzed the anger associated response to the stress during adult life. The study observed that men with the highest levels of heart problems had earlier experienced concealed or expressed anger and irritability as young adults. Remember that easily angered people don't always curse and throw things; sometimes they withdraw socially, sulk, or get physically ill. Even if you are right some of the times there is nothing much to be gained by your self becoming angry and adversarial with your family and friends. Tough times need cool and composed attitudes and not temporary moments of aggression, resentment and hatred. Words are like bullets, once shot, they are impossible to retrieve, so please choose them with care, caution and thought.

*When you are finding yourself reacting with anger or opposition to any person or circumstance, realize that you are only struggling with yourself. When you relinquish this anger, you are healing yourself.*

— *Deepak Chopra*

The goal of anger management is to reduce both your emotional feelings and the physiological arousal that anger causes. You can not avoid the things or the people that enrage you, nor can you change them, but you can certainly learn to control your responses and reactions. Don't let a few bad apples flip you off. You may win the battle but you could lose the metaphorical war.

Learning effective anger management strategies adds to your peace and happiness by helping you redirect your energies towards more creative and positive pursuits. Simple relaxation tools, such as deep breathing and relaxing imagery can help you to calm down angry feelings. Books and CD ROMs can teach you relaxation techniques. If you are involved in a relationship where both partners are hot headed it might be a good idea for both of you to learn these techniques.

It is a good strategy to wait briefly to count upto ten to prevent an angry outburst. Angry people tend to jump on impressions and conclusions, and some of those are much farther away from the truth. The first thing to do if you're in a heated discussion is slow down and think through your responses. If you are angry, try to talk more quietly and softly than you usually do. Don't say the first thing that comes into your head, instead slow down and think carefully about what you want to say. At the same time, listen carefully to what the other person is saying and take your time before answering.

If you are angry with your spouse, make it a point to resolve the differences before going to bed. The Bible very rightly teaches – Let the sun not go down on your anger. Remind yourself that getting angry is not going to fix anything that it won't make you feel better in any way what so ever. Simply put, this means changing the way you think. This strategy is referred to as cognitive restructuring.

Taming your anger and aggression can be a challenging task and you need some time to do that. It is not practical to expect immediate results so please give yourself some time to effectively put into practice desirable changes in your reactions. Switch on your mind to something else. You would agree that losing your temper, getting even or blowing your stack may look alright at the time, but it almost always makes the things worse. As the saying goes, he who angers you, conquers you. Conquer the anger before it gets hold of you.

## CHPATER FORTY SEVEN

# DO YOUR SWOT ANALYSIS

*Obstacles don't have to stop you. If you run into a wall, don't turn around and give up. Figure out how to climb it, go through it or work around it.*

— *Michael Jordon*

A popular, imaginary and an inspiring story draws attention to noteworthy aspects of strengths, perseverance and an attitude of never say die. One of the milk vendors in a city ferried his milk in the cans on his motor bike, waking up his morning customers with a pleasant smile. One day some naughty boys put one frog each in his two milk cans. One of these two frogs started feeling low, scared and tense. The frog blamed himself that he was very small and couldn't do anything to get out of the can and ultimately drowned himself in the milk. The other frog in the other can realized his strength of swimming, and he knew that difficult times do not last long. He started jumping with all his might in the milk. Soon he was sitting on the lump of butter formed due to the churning caused by his swimming. As soon as the can was opened, he jumped away to freedom.

*Action is the antidote to despair.*

*— Joan Baez*

Similar to the happy frog, the human mind should be open to perform the SWOT

(Strengths, Weaknesses, Opportunities and Threats) analysis. The second frog utilized his strength to swim and churn the butter and got an opportunity to freedom. If you want God to help you, create a positive attitude, make your own SWOT analysis and do the best. There are fair chances that you would come out tougher from life's adversities. Remember John Neal's inspiration– *Kites rise against, not with the wind.*

Whether there are glad tidings or stormy weather – life continues to move on and gives us hope and faith to hold on. Occasionally you are going to miss a shot but most of the times you will hit correctly. Don't let a setback discourage you from seeking a way to overcome an obstacle. The secret is to keep trying. Seek help. Seek advice. Seek counsel from friends and elders. Robert Schuler has written a punch line– *Tough times don't last but tough people do.* Treat difficulties as lessons and use opportunities to be recognized as solution.

## CHAPTER FORTY EIGHT

# MEDITATION, A DELIGHT

*My concern is with growth. You must grow to become one, to become whole, to become sane. I am going to bring out your insanity. When it is pulled out completely, thrown into the wind, sanity will happen to you, you will grow. You will be transformed. That is the meaning of meditation.*

– *Osho*

The Oxford Dictionary Thesaurus gives different meanings to the word meditation – cerebration, contemplation, deliberation, musing, prayer, reflection, rumination, thought and yoga. Basic techniques for contacting the subconscious mind and harnessing it's power have been a standard part of people's culture. Dr. Bernie Siegel defines meditation very appropriately – as a method by which we can temporarily stop listening to the pressures and distractions of every day life and thereby are able to acknowledge other things, such as deep thoughts, the peace of pure consciousness and spiritual awareness.

Meditation helps us to focus our minds in a state of relaxed awareness leading to enlightenment, calmness filling us with positive energy and genuine inner peace and happiness. It is about experiencing your body and mind in the present moment. Meditation besides enlightening us for health and happiness also helps relieve us of maladies like anxiety, depression, and sleeplessness. Research at University of Wisconsin has found that people who practiced meditation regularly had higher levels of disease fighting antibodies in their blood. Scientists have also discovered that during meditation, the body increases its release of a number of happiness hormones. We can mediate for five minutes or fifty, day or night, at home or at work and have it's good effects.

While it may be transcendental meditation, breath awareness, tai chi or yoga, all these techniques help you to bring forth a relaxation response. To begin, it does need some effort and it may be challenging to stick with it. Find a yoga class or books or VCDs/DVDs to make a beginning. The peace and tranquility that you would feel after fifteen to twenty minutes of daily meditation will infuse every remaining minute of the day. One of the popularly practiced muscle relaxation techniques according to Jacobson is called progressive relaxation. This method, which is also used by psychotherapists for the treatment of anxiety disorders contributes to the inner peace first by tensing the individual muscle areas of the body and then relaxing them.

Yoga is a relaxation method where you have to concentrate by performing certain exercises correctly in harmony with your breathing. Yoga may be referred to as "Your Own Guru Always"! Tai chi too is a wonderful relaxation method for those who like to relax by the movements. Practice meditating once a day and supplement it with mini medits. Sitting in your office or while waiting for a meeting, quietly close your eyes, take a few deep breaths and meditate for a few minutes. There is nothing like meditation to have the calm and perspective to gain control of the mind. How about sitting back for a few moments, closing your eyes and experiencing a state of tranquility and deep relaxation ?

# CHAPTER FORTY NINE

# LIFE IS AN ATTITUDE

*The ability to do anything must be accompanied by the belief that we can do it.*

*– David Niven*

One of the fundamental aspects that is going to determine your life's ultimate satisfaction and happiness is your attitude and ability to believe in yourself. We are faced by common questions— what do we think about life? What are our concerns? What are our hopes? What are our fears? What are our goals? We need to believe firmly in our potentials, strengths and capabilities. Life itself is a never ending education. Let your experiences and endurances become your teacher.

Passion is the key word if you want to discover the spirit of entrepreneurship within you. The beauty of entrepreneurship and passion is that you can go on doing what you love to do; cherish and enjoy it until you want to. Winning does not come easily – it needs striving in form of hard work, perseverance, honesty, motivation and commitment.

*People who say it can not be done, should not interrupt those who are doing it.*

*— Anonymous*

Walt Disney left Kansas City for Hollywood in 1923 with $40 in his pocket, some drawing material and a complete animation film. Disneyland was launched in 1955 and has entertained more than three hundred million people by it's third decade. Disney and his creations continue to touch the hearts and minds of millions of children and adults all over the world. The realization of Bill Gates vision has changed the computing world in the last twenty years. Dr. Naresh Trehan of Escorts Heart Institute had his life shaped by partition of India in 1947. Don't dream your life away but live your dreams.

The person you want to become in a few years from now is up to you. You have a potential to grow, develop and manifest yourself totally. Let every corner of your soul radiantly blossom forth . Take control of your life, set goals and break them into short term targets. Go ahead in building your accomplishments slowly and steadily. Believe in yourself, perform at the best of your capabilities, keep up your self-motivation and be happy. Passion is the spark that ignites self motivation. Don't think that you will not make a mistake but keep learning and don't write yourself off. Never!

# CHAPTER FIFTY

# SUBMIT TO SPIRITUAL SPLENDOR

*The life of a man is a precious gift that must be loved and defended in all its stages: the commandment "thou shalt not kill," he said, "calls for life to be respected from its beginning until its natural twilight."*

— *Pope John Paul II*

Prayers are offerings to what is greater than one-self. It's a humbling effect that restores tranquility to the mind. Spirituality is the being of spirit. Every time I pray, I feel there is a supreme being above who controls everything. A balance between my emotional and spiritual plane allows me to live with harmony. Spirituality is a way to sensitize oneself to the concerns and well being of fellow human beings and a means to bring life and livelihood back together again in a better way. Spirituality and religious faith soothe my psyche at home, workplace and in the community. A recent survey showed that 95% of the Americans say they believe in God or a universal spirit. People now believe that spirituality makes them experience an eternal bliss, immense benediction and enhanced dimensions of wisdom. Spirituality is the manifestation of the perfection that is already there within you. It has no religious component or preference; it is a way of expressing more humanity. Spirituality brings back our vision and awakening of true emotions, moods and feelings.

Spirituality offers us faith, strength, hope and answers to many of our unresolved questions. It often goes beyond human explanations. There have been times in our lives when only faith has sustained us through those hard times.

Twenty years ago, Nitin Mohite was a dynamic government executive in mid forties when he suffered the first attack of chest pain. An angiography revealed multiple blocks in his coronary arteries and subsequently he underwent coronary artery bypass surgery and later again an angioplasty within ten years. Besides angioplasty, during this duration he developed heart rhythm disturbances and by usual medical dictum he may not have been alive today. Instead he is now nearly seventy years old, walks regularly, travels outstation to visit his grandchildren and lives a spiritual and healthy life. He firmly attributes his health and well being to the spiritual and religious faith. One may feel skeptic about such a thing but research at Harvard Medical School, USA, backs his beliefs and concludes that active religious practices are associated with longer, happier and healthier lives. No wonder, one of the important reason behind the health and longevity of our saints and priests is their unflinching belief and practice of spirituality and religion.

*Spiritual beings keep their thoughts focused on love and harmony.*

*— Wayne W Dyer*

Whether we go to temples, mosques or churches or read the religious scriptures or become compassionate and helpful human beings, the supreme power high up and above is there to help, support, guide and bless all of us. Follow the spiritual path, begin to live with spiritual splendor and thus live your lives happily.

# Suggested Further Reading

1. Robin Sharma. The Greatness. Jaico Publishing House. New Delhi, 2006.
2. David Niven. The 100 Simple Secrets of Happy People. Harper. San Francisco, 2000.
3. Richard Carlson. Don't Sweat the Small Stuff With the Family. Hodder and Slaughten. London, 1998.
4. Stephen Covey. The Seven Habits of Highly Effective People. Franklin Covey Co. New York, 2004.
5. Gael Lindonfield. Short Cuts To Finding Your Get Up and Go. Thorsons. London, 2002.
6. Geet Sethi. Success Versus Joy. Media. New Delhi, 2004.

7. David Possen. The Little Book of Stress Relief. Jaico Publishing House. Mumbai, 2006.

8. Pramod Batra. Cows Don't Give Milk. Full Circle. New Delhi, 2003.

9. Paul Hanna. You Can Do It. Penguin India. New Delhi, 2000.

10. Andrew Matthews. Happiness Now. Seashell Publishers, Queensland, 2005.